# The Essence of Other-Emptiness

# The Essence of Other-Emptiness

## Tāranātha

Translated and Annotated by Jeffrey Hopkins
In collaboration with Lama Lodrö Namgyel

Snow Lion Publications
Ithaca, New York
Boulder, Colorado

Snow Lion Publications
P.O. Box 6483
Ithaca, NY 14851 USA
(607) 273-8519
www.snowlionpub.com



Printed in USA on acid-free recycled paper.

ISBN-10: 1-55939-273-8
ISBN-13: 978-1-55939-273-0

*Library of Congress Cataloging-in-Publication Data*

Tāranātha, Jo-naṅ-pa, b. 1575.
[Gźan stoṅ sñiṅ po. English]
The essence of other-emptiness / Taranatha ; translated and annotated by Jeffrey Hopkins in collaboration with Lama Lodro Namgyel.
p. cm.
Includes English translation of Zab don gñer gcig pa as supplementary text.
Includes bibliographical references.
ISBN-13: 978-1-55939-273-0 (alk. paper)
ISBN-10: 1-55939-273-8 (alk. paper)
1. Jo-naṅ-pa (Sect)--Doctrines--Early works to 1800. 2. Sunyata--Early works to 1800. I. Tāranātha, Jo-naṅ-pa, b. 1575. Zab don gñer gcig pa. English. II. Hopkins, Jeffrey. III. Lodro Namgyel. IV. Title.
BQ7674.4.T36 2007
294.3'420423--dc22

2006034379

# Contents

# Technical Notes

Please notice that:

- Full bibliographical references are given in the footnotes at first citation.
- For translations and editions of texts, see the Bibliography.
- The names of Indian Buddhist schools are translated into English in an effort to increase accessibility for non-specialists.
- For the names of Indian scholars and systems cited in the body of the text, *ch, sh,* and *ṣh* are used instead of the more usual *c, ś,* and *ṣ* for the sake of easy pronunciation by non-specialists; however, *cch* is used for *cch,* not *chchh.* In parentheses the usual transliteration system for Sanskrit is used.
- Transliteration of Tibetan is done in accordance with a system devised by Turrell Wylie; see "A Standard System of Tibetan Transcription," *Harvard Journal of Asiatic Studies* 22 (1959): 261-267,
- The names of Tibetan authors and orders are given in "essay phonetics" for the sake of easy pronunciation. The system is used consistently, with the result that a few well-known names are rendered in a different way; for example, "Lhasa" is rendered as "Hla-s̄a," since the letter "h" is pronounced before the letter "l." In the table below, the Wylie transliteration form of Tibetan letters is on the left of each column and my "essay phonetics" form is on the right.

| | | | |
|---|---|---|---|
| ka = ḡa | kha = ka | ga = ga | nga = nga or n̄ga[a] |
| ca = j̄ | cha = cha | ja = ja | nya = nya or n̄ya |
| ta = d̄a | tha = ta | da = da | na = na or n̄a |
| pa = b̄a | pha = pa | ba = ba | ma = ma or m̄a |
| tsa = d̄za | tsha = tsa | dza = dza | wa = wa |
| zha = sha | za = sa | 'a = a | ya = ya |
| ra = ra | la = la | sha = s̄ha | sa = s̄a |
| ha = ha | a = a | | |

[a] Nasals (*nga, nya, na, ma*) in the root position take on a high tone only when affected by a prefixed or superscribed letter.

# Introduction

Tāranātha was born in 1575 in a family descended from the famous Translator Gya Dor-jay-sang-b̄o (*rgya lo tsā ba rdo rje bzang po*) in an area between the two major provinces of central Tibet.[a] At birth he was given the name Ḡün-ga-ñying-b̄o (*kun dga' snying po*), meaning "Essence of Total Joy." The name Tāranātha (*sgrol ba'i mgon po*) itself means "Liberating-Protector," and Gareth Sparham[b] speculates that his preference for this "Sanskrit form of the honorific title reflects the importance he gave to his knowledge of Sanskrit, and to his contacts with pilgrims from western India." Sparham points out Tāranātha wrote many

> works on the *Kālachakra Tantra* and *Cakrasaṃvara Tantra* in particular, and also translated a book on grammar, the *Sarasvatavyākaraṇa*[c] into Tibetan...he met and studied with—besides Buddhagupta-[nātha], Premānanda and Pūrṇānanda, etc.—the learned Sanskrit grammarian paṇḍita Kṛṣṇa of Varaṇāsī. This connection with Indian religious figures is unusual at so late a period of Tibetan history.

Tāranātha's vast writings are contained in twenty-three volumes, several of which have been translated. His famed *History of Buddhism in India,* written in 1608 at age thirty-four, was translated Russian by V.P. Vasil'ev in 1869 and into German by A. Schiefner in the same year, and into English by E. Obermiller in 1932 and Lama Chimpa and Alaka Chattopadhyaya in 1970. His *Story of the Lineage Endowed with Seven Transmissions,*[d] biographical sketches of fifty-nine tāntrikas, was first translated into German by Grünwedel in 1914 and into English by David Templeman in

---

a That is, between *dbus* and *gtsang.*

b The citation is taken from the introduction in Gareth Sparham's unpublished translation of Tāranātha's *rgyud rgyal gshin rje gshed skor gyi chos 'byung rgyas pa yid ches ngo mtshar.*

c This is by Anubhūtisvarūpācārya; see the Bibliography.

d *bka' babs bdun ldan gyi brgyud pa'i rnam thar.*

1983. His *Long History of the Yamāntaka-Tantra-Rāja Cycle [Called "Causing] Wondrous Belief,"*[a] written in 1631, has been translated into English by Gareth Sparham but not yet published. His *Essence of Ambrosia* has been translated into English by Willa Baker in 2005.[b] His *Twenty-one Differences Regarding the Profound Meaning,* which contrasts the views of Shākya Chok-den[c] and Döl-b̄o-b̄a S̄hay-rap-gyel-tsen,[d] has been translated into English by Klaus-Dieter Mathes in 2004[e] and is the supplementary text translated in the present book.

Tāranātha was recognized as the fourteenth[f] in a long line of reincarnations, among whom was Jam-ȳang-chö-jay,[g] the Ge-luk-b̄a[h] savant who founded Dre-b̄ung[i] Monastic University in the Hla-s̄a[j] area in 1416, which eventually became the largest educational institution in Tibet with over ten thousand members before the Chinese Communist invasion in 1959. Jam-ȳang-chö-jay's writings evince a penchant for the Jo-nang-b̄a doctrine of other-emptiness and were controversial in Ge-luk-b̄a circles.

At the Jo-nang seat in Jo-mo-nang, in 1615 Tāranātha founded a monastery named Permanent Stable Wonderful Land (*rtag brtan phun tshogs gling*). Later, in the midst of political turmoil it was taken over by the government of the Fifth Dalai Lama and converted into a Ge-luk-b̄a monastery. As Gareth Sparham says:

The later suppression of the Jo nang pa school in general,

---

a *rgyud rgyal gshin rje gshed skor gyi chos 'byung rgyas pa yid ches ngo mtshar.*

b Dharamsala, India: Library of Tibetan Works and Archives, 2005.

c *shākya mchog ldan,* 1428-1507.

d *dol po pa* (also *dol bu pa*) *shes rab rgyal mtshan,* 1292-1361.

e Klaus-Dieter Mathes, "Tāranātha's Twenty-one Differences with Regard to the Profound Meaning," *Journal of the International Association of Buddhist Studies,* vol. 27, no. 2 (2004): 285-328.

f Or perhaps the sixteenth.

g *'jam dbyangs chos rje,* 1379-1449.

h *dge lugs pa.*

i *'bras spungs.*

j *lha sa.*

and of Tāranātha's works in particular, by the emergent dGe lugs pas under their leader the Fifth Dalai Lama cannot be traced to any injunction in the works of Tsong kha pa or his immediate disciples. One suspects the consolidation of power over central Tibet and the need to retain the undivided loyalty of powerful Mongolian backers better explains why it occurred...

The death of Yon tan rGya mTsho, the fourth Dalai bLa ma in 1616, brings us to the time of Tāranātha. We know that Tāranātha, like other learned and religious Tibetans, was also courted by Mongolians seeking religious knowledge. It is even said that during this period, which marks the final chapter in the struggle between the bKa' brGyud and the gTsang Princes on the one side and the dGe lugs pa on the other, Tāranātha spent more than twenty years teaching and establishing monasteries in Mongolia. The extent to which he was held in high regard by a section of the Mongolians is shown by the fact that he was known as rJe brTsun dam pa ("Holy Lord") and after his death his reincarnations as the Khal kha rJe brTsun dam pas continued in Mongolia down into the twentieth century. Not only this, but, as mentioned earlier, Tāranātha was also connected with the last of the great rulers of gTsang, the Rin sPungs prince Karma bsTan sKyong dBang po, who had supplied him with the means to build his own monastery and reprint many of the important Jo nang pa works. It is scarcely surprising, therefore, that when soon after the death of Tāranātha...Karma bsTan sKyong dBang po was defeated by Gu shri khan on behalf of the fifth Dalai Lama, Tāranātha's monastery, so closely associated with the ruler of gTsang and a possible focus of Mongolian devotion, was turned into a dGe lugs pa monastery, and the views of the Jo nang pa sect which were championed by Tāranātha condemned as the worst heresy. The Glorious Fifth and his advisors wanted to take no chances with another power center developing in gTsang, particularly when it was associated with a scholarly and religious figure much loved by many Mongolians. To declare

> the views of the sect antithetical to those of Tsong kha pa, and by extension to the Dalai Lamas who had inherited his spiritual mantle, was a draconian measure no doubt, but it was a sure way to prevent their further spread amongst the Mongolians which might sway them from unwavering and single-pointed support.

Tāranātha died in Mongolia in 1634 in the Wood Dog year, taking rebirth in 1635 there as L̄o-sang-d̄en-b̄ay-gyel-tsen,[a] the fifteenth[b] in the line of his reincarnations.

As Willa Baker reports, "Tāranātha's life example so inspired Jamgon Kongtrul that he devoted three days a year in his retreat center to the celebration of Tāranātha's memory, an honor he extended to no other single lineage holder."

## THE TEXT: *THE ESSENCE OF OTHER-EMPTINESS*

In the Jo-nang-b̄a sect of Tibetan Buddhism, Döl-b̄o-b̄a S̄hay-rap-gyel-tsen and Tāranātha are recognized as its two leading exponents. Döl-b̄o-b̄a is commonly called "Omniscient" (*kun mkhyen*), and Tāranātha is commonly called "Holy Leader" (*rje btsun*). Döl-b̄o-b̄a wrote what became the fundamental text of the system, his *Mountain Doctrine, Ocean of Definitive Meaning: Final Unique Quintessential Instructions.*[c] In this massive treatise he authenticates the doctrine of other-emptiness through citing a huge number of Indian scriptural sources and through presenting an elaborate argument establishing other-emptiness, and not self-emptiness, as the ultimate. Three centuries later, Tāranātha's concise *The Essence of Other-Emptiness*[d] places the doctrine of other-emptiness in the context of schools of tenets, primarily the famed four schools of Buddhist India, while also mentioning three non-Buddhist schools.

---

[a] *blo bzang bstan pa'i rgyal mtshan,* 1635-1723.

[b] Or perhaps the seventeenth.

[c] *ri chos nges don rgya mtsho zhes bya ba mthar thug thun mong ma yin pa'i man ngag.* For a complete translation see Jeffrey Hopkins, *Mountain Doctrine: Tibet's Fundamental Treatise on Other-Emptiness and the Buddha Matrix* (Ithaca, N.Y.: Snow Lion Publications, 2006).

[d] *gzhan stong snying po.* For the two editions used, see the Bibliography.

Non-Buddhist Schools

Lokāyata[a] (Hedonists)

Sāṃkhya[b] (Enumerators)

Nirgrantha[c] (The Unclothed), also known as Jaina[d] (Followers of Jina)

Buddhist Schools

*Lesser Vehicle* (*hīnayāna*)[e]

1. Great Exposition School[f]
2. Sūtra School[g]

*Great Vehicle* (*mahāyāna*)

3. Mind-Only School[h]
4. Middle Way School[i]
   - Ordinary Middle Way[j]
   - Great Middle Way[k]

---

a *rgyang 'phan pa.*

b *grangs can pa.*

c *gcer bu pa.*

d *rgyal ba pa.*

e The term "Lesser Vehicle" (*theg dman, hīnayāna*) has its origin in the writings of Great Vehicle (*theg chen, mahāyāna*) authors and was, of course, not used by those to whom it was ascribed. Substitutes such as "non-Great Vehicle," "Nikāya Buddhism," and "Theravādayāna" have been suggested in order to avoid the pejorative sense of "Lesser." However, "Lesser Vehicle" is a convenient term in this particular context for a type of tenet system or practice that is seen, in the tradition presented in this book, to be surpassed—but not negated—by a higher system. The "Lesser Vehicle" is not despised, most of it being incorporated into the "Great Vehicle." The monks' and nuns' vows are Lesser Vehicle, as is much of the course of study in Tibetan monastic circles. ("Lesser Vehicle" and "Low Vehicle" are used interchangeably in this book.)

f *bye brag smra ba, vaibhāṣika.*

g *mdo sde pa, sautrāntika.*

h *sems tsam pa, cittamātra.*

i *dbu ma pa, mādhyamika.*

j *dbu ma phal pa.*

k *dbu ma chen po.*

Tāranātha's text compartmentalizes schools by way of philosophical perspective in a Buddhist tradition that dates back to Indian works such as the *Blaze of Reasoning*[a] by Bhāvaviveka (500-570? C.E.) and the *Compendium of Principles*[b] by the eighth-century scholar Shāntarakṣhita, with a commentary by his student Kamalashīla, both of whom visited Tibet. In Tibet itself there were lengthy presentations such as the *Precious Treasury of Tenets: Illuminating the Meaning of All Vehicles*[c] by the fourteenth-century scholar Long-chen-rap-jam[d] of the Nying-ma sect, Dzong-ka-ba's[e] *The Essence of Eloquence*[f] of the Ge-luk-ba sect, and the *Explanation of "Freedom from Extremes through Understanding All Tenets": Ocean of Eloquence*[g] by the fifteenth-century scholar Dak-tsang Shay-rap-rin-

---

a *rtog ge 'bar ba, tarkajvālā.* This is Bhāvaviveka's commentary on his *Heart of the Middle* (*dbu ma'i snying po, madhyamakahṛdaya*). For a partial English translation of the latter (chap. III, 1-136), see Shōtarō Iida, *Reason and Emptiness* (Tokyo: Hokuseido, 1980).

b *de kho na nyid bsdud pa'i tshig le'ur byas pa, tattvasaṃgrahakārikā.* A translation into English is available in G. Jha, *The Tattvasaṃgraha of Śāntirakṣita, with the Commentary of Kamalaśīla*, Gaekwad's Oriental Series, vols. 80 and 83 (Baroda, India: Oriental Institute, 1937-1939; rpt. Delhi: Motilal Banarsidass, 1986).

c *theg pa mtha' dag gi don gsal bar byed pa grub pa'i mtha' rin po che'i mdzod.*

d *klong chen rab 'byams / klong chen dri med 'od zer,* 1308-1363.

e *tsong kha pa blo bzang grags pa,* 1357-1419.

f *drang ba dang nges pa'i don rnam par phye ba'i bstan bcos legs bshad snying po;* P6142, vol. 153. My annotated translation of the General Explanation and the Section on the Mind-Only School is to be found in *Emptiness in the Mind-Only School of Buddhism* (Berkeley: University of California Press, 1999). For a translation of the complete text, see Robert A. F. Thurman, *Tsong Khapa's Speech of Gold in the Essence of True Eloquence* (Princeton, N.J.: Princeton University Press, 1984). A Chinese translation was completed in Hla-sa on the day commemorating Buddha's enlightenment in 1916 by Venerable Fa Zun, "Bian Liao Yi Bu Liao Yi Shuo Cang Lun," in *Xi Zang Fo Jiao Jiao Yi Lun Ji* (Taipei: Da Sheng Wen Hua Chu Ban She, 1979), vol. 2, 159-276.

g *grub mtha' kun shes nas mtha' bral grub pa zhes bya ba'i bstan bcos rnam par bshad pa legs bshad kyi rgya mtsho.*

chen[a] of the S̄a-ḡya sect. Tāranātha's text is in the tradition of brief presentations of tenets, such as those found in Jay-d̄zün Chö-ḡyi-gyel-tsen's[b] *Presentation of Tenets,*[c] the Second Dalai Lama Ge-dün-gya-tso's[d] *Ship for Entering the Ocean of Tenets,*[e] and Paṇ-chen S̄ö-nam-drak-b̄a's[f] *Presentation of Tenets: Sublime Tree Inspiring Those of Clear Mind, Hammer Destroying the Stone Mountains of Opponents.*[g] These brief presentations provide a valuable way for students to gain an overview of their respective school's outlook without being overwhelmed by source quotes and extended arguments.

As Tāranātha's title, *The Essence of Other-Emptiness,* indicates, his specific intention is to focus, though not exclusively, on tenets that serve to highlight the special doctrine of other-emptiness in the highest system, the Great Middle Way, through comparing other schools' opinions on the status of the noumenon[h] and phenomena.[i] A central point is the position of each of the schools on true establishment (*bden par grub pa*).[j] (See chart next page.)

The Sūtra School and above do not make a distinction between true existence and true establishment, but the Great Exposition School holds that all phenomena are truly established but only individual minute particles and individual moments of consciousnesses are truly existent; gross objects composed of particles as well as continuums composed of moments of consciousness are not

---

a *stag tshang lo tsā ba shes rab rin chen,* b. 1405.

b *rje btsun chos kyi rgyal mtshan,* 1469-1546.

c *grub mtha'i rnam gzhag.*

d *dge 'dun rgya mtsho,* 1476-1542.

e *grub mtha' rgya mtshor 'jug pa'i gru rdzings.*

f *paṇ chen bsod nams grags pa,* 1478-1554.

g *grub mtha'i rnam bzhag blo gsal spro ba bskyed pa'i ljon pa phas rgol brag ri 'joms pa'i tho ba.* For a list of other such brief texts, see the Bibliography in Katsumi Mimaki, *Blo gsal grub mtha'* (Kyoto: Université de Kyoto, 1982), p. XLVI, etc., as well as the Introduction, pp. 5-12.

h *chos nyid, dharmatā.*

i *chos, dharma.*

j Döl-b̄o-b̄a does not use the vocabulary of true establishment and true existence except in rare instances. Rather, he speaks of ultimate establishment (*don dam par grub pa*) and ultimate existence (*don dam par yod pa*).

| *School* | *Truly established* | *Existing but not truly established* |
|---|---|---|
| Great Exposition | all phenomena—compounded and uncompounded, conventional and ultimate | |
| Sūtra | present minute particles<br>present moments of consciousness | gross objects<br>continuums<br>uncompounded phenomena<br>non-associated compositional factors |
| Mind-Only | consciousness devoid of apprehended-object and apprehending-subject | continuums<br>uncompounded phenomena<br>non-associated compositional factors |
| Ordinary Middle Way | | all phenomena—compounded and uncompounded, conventional and ultimate |
| Great Middle Way | matrix-of-One-Gone-Thus<br>self-cognizing, self-illuminating pristine wisdom<br>all ultimate Buddha-qualities primordially in-dwelling intrinsically<br>other-emptiness<br>immutable thoroughly established nature | all compounded phenomena<br>all adventitiously posited uncompounded phenomena<br>self-emptiness |

truly existent. The movement up the ladder of tenets is through greater and greater denial of true establishment, until in the Ordinary Middle Way School it goes too far, even denying the true establishment of the ultimate, the noumenon. This is corrected in the Great Middle Way through asserting that ultimate truth—also called self-arisen pristine wisdom, matrix-of-One-Gone-Thus, and so forth—is truly established.

## THE SUPPLEMENTARY TEXT: *TWENTY-ONE DIFFERENCES REGARDING THE PROFOUND MEANING*

In the *Twenty-one Differences Regarding the Profound Meaning*[a] Tāranātha presents opinions of a prominent fifteenth-century scholar of the S̄a-ḡya sect, Shākya Chok-den,[b] and then counters these with the favored views of the fourteenth-century primary expositor of his own Jo-nang-b̄a sect, Döl-b̄o-b̄a S̄hay-rap-gyel-tsen. About Shākya Chok-den's place among fifteenth-century S̄a-ḡya thinkers, Yaroslav Komarovski says:[c]

> Shākya Chokden (*gser mdog paṇchen śākya mchog ldan,* 1428-1507) was educated in the Sakya tradition of Tibetan Buddhism under Rongtön Sheja Kunrik (*rong ston shes bya kun rig,* 1367-1449 ), Ngorchen Kunga Sangpo (*ngor chen kun dga' bzang po,* 1382-1456), and other important thinkers of the fifteenth century. His writings contributed to many areas, such as logic and epistemology, Buddhist history, bridging tantric and non-tantric views, theories of perception, etc.
>
> Within the Sakya tradition, Gorampa Sonam Senge (*go ram pa bsod nams seng ge,* 1429-1489) is considered to be the most influential philosopher of the past five centuries by far. Yet during his lifetime Gorampa's influence was closely rivaled by that of Shākya Chokden, whose works until recently received little or no attention among modern

---

[a] *zab don khyad par nyer gcig pa,* also called *zab don nyer gcig pa.*

[b] *gser mdog paṇ chen shākya mchog ldan,* 1428-1507. For Shākya Chok-den's criticism of D̄zong-ka-b̄a's views, see Iaroslav Komarovski, *Three Texts on Madhyamaka* (Dharamsala: Library of Tibetan Works and Archives, 2000). See also David Seyfort Ruegg, "The Jo naṅ pas: A School of Buddhist Ontologists According to the Grub mtha' šel gyi me loṅ," *Journal of the American Oriental Society* 83, no. 1 (1963): 89-90.

[c] With his permission, these remarks have been cobbled together from Yaroslav Komarovski, "Slicing the Pie Alternatively: Śākya mchog ldan on Divisions of the Mahāyāna Tenets," a paper presented at the annual AAR conference in Washington, D.C., 2006, and Iaroslav Komarovski (trans. and introduction), *Three Texts on Madhyamaka,* ix.

> scholars.
>
> Although the views of Shākya Chokden and Gorampa often differ greatly on many points of Madhyamaka, their contribution was similar in that they both greatly clarified the views of their own tradition through numerous commentaries on Indian and Tibetan treatises, and also through their original treatises and critical texts aimed at the views of Tsongkhapa (*tsong kha pa,* 1357-1419) and his followers, known as Gelukpa.
>
> The lineage of most of Gorampa's works, which are traditionally transmitted orally through reading and explanation, has survived unbroken until the present day. However, the lineage of transmission of Shākya Chokden's works was broken. Shākya Chokden's works commanded a lesser following because many Sakyapas, facing the problem of whether to follow Gorampa or Shākya Chokden, had chosen to follow the former, since, according to many Sakya scholars, his approach more correctly expresses the views held by Sakya Paṇḍita Kunga Gyaltsen (*sa skya paṇḍita kun dga' rgyal mtshan,* 1182-1251), the supreme authority of Sakya tradition, and other Sakya masters of the past.

Given Shākya Chok-den's importance in the fifteenth and sixteenth centuries and his opposition to many of Döl-b̄o-b̄a's view, Tāranātha formulated a debate between these two masters. Tāranātha sees all of the twenty-one differences as stemming from the single topic of the nature of non-dual pristine wisdom,[a] which Shākya Chok-den takes to be impermanent and Döl-b̄o-b̄a takes to be permanent (132):

> Concerning those, the reasons for the arising of that many different incidental assertions mostly stem from one root. What is that one? The paṇḍita named Shākya asserts that non-dual pristine wisdom has a nature not of singularity but of multiplicity and is impermanent, not abiding for an instant. The Omniscient Jo-nang-b̄a asserts that although

[a] *gnyis med ye shes.*

non-dual pristine wisdom is indeed definite in actual fact as not one or many, for the time being he takes a presentation of it as singular to be correct, since it is asserted as being partless, all-pervasive, devoid of proliferation, and devoid of predication. In brief, they differ in asserting it to be impermanent and permanent.

In the course of his exposition, Tāranātha explains that according to Döl-b̄o-b̄a self-arisen pristine wisdom:

- withstands analysis by the reasoning of dependent-arising, the lack of being one or many, and so forth and hence is truly existent
- is an established base[a] but neither an effective thing nor a non-thing, both of which are necessarily conventionalities and compounded
- is cognition[b] but neither an effective thing nor a non-thing, both of which are necessarily conventionalities
- is partless and all-pervasive
- is permanent and steady and is the *actual* uncompounded and thus is not impermanent, momentary, or compounded, even though others claim that non-things are uncompounded.

Near the end of this text Tāranātha, sensitive to problems involved in explaining what it means for self-arisen pristine wisdom to be permanent and yet be neither an effective thing nor a non-thing, approaches the issue first by detailing what it does not mean. About real permanence[c] he says that:

- It is not just the mere opposite of impermanence, which would be a permanent non-thing.[d]
- It is also not what non-Buddhist Forders assert to be a permanent effective thing,[e] which does not even occur among objects of knowledge. (This does not imply that self-arisen

---

a *gzhi grub.*

b *shes pa.*

c *yang dag pa'i rtag pa.*

d *mi rtag pa log tsam gyi rtag pa dngos med.*

e *rtag dngos.*

pristine wisdom is not an object of knowledge, for, as Döl-b̄o-b̄a clearly says,[a] it is.)
- It is also not a case of calling a never-ending continuum "permanent,"[b] which actually is compounded and not permanent, since it is uncompounded.
- It is also not a negative permanence that is a mere meaning-generality.[c] (This does not imply that self-arisen pristine wisdom is not a negative, since Döl-b̄o-b̄a repeatedly says[d] that other-emptiness is an affirming negative.)
- It is also not a positive self-powered permanence.[e]

Then, Tāranātha declares that self-arisen pristine wisdom is the immutable basic element[f] released from the proliferations of impermanent positive effective things[g] and negative permanent non-things.[h] Nevertheless, it is immutable[i] and hence solely-permanent,[j] a term reminiscent of N̄ying-ma teachings that the great completeness[k] is a "great permanence,"[l] a term intended to

---

a See *Mountain Doctrine,* 33-35.

b *rgyun gyi rtag pa.*

c *dgag pa'i rtag pa don spyi tsam.*

d See *Mountain Doctrine,* 22.

e *sgrub pa rang dbang can gyi rtag pa.* The objection here is perhaps to "self-powered," since Döl-b̄o-b̄a (*Mountain Doctrine,* 470, 535) speaks of positive attributes in the ultimate.

f *dbyings.*

g *dngos po sgrub pa mi rtag pa.*

h *dngos med dgag pa rtag pa.*

i *mi 'gyur ba.*

j *rtag pa kho na.*

k *rdzogs pa chen po.*

l *rtag pa chen po.* For instance, Mi-pam-gya-tso says, "...the body of pristine wisdom—a great permanence like a vajra never fluctuating from the sphere of reality—is a great uncompoundedness; it is not compounded." See *The Meaning of Fundamental Mind, Clear Light, Expressed in Accordance with the Transmission of Conqueror Knowledge-Bearers: Vajra Matrix* (*gnyug sems 'od gsal gyi don rgyal ba rig 'dzin brgyud pa'i lung bzhin brjod pa rdo rje'i snying po*) presented in Mi-pam-gya-tso, *Fundamental Mind: The Nyingma View of the Great Completeness,* with commentary by

raise this type of permanence above the dual category of impermanence and permanence.

I wish to express my gratitude to Yaroslav Komarovski for making many helpful suggestions concerning the translation of Tāranātha's *Twenty-one Differences Regarding the Profound Meaning.*

Jeffrey Hopkins
Emeritus Professor of Tibetan Studies
University of Virginia

Khetsun Sangbo Rinbochay, trans. and ed. by Jeffrey Hopkins (Ithaca, N.Y.: Snow Lion Publications, 2006), 132.

# *The Essence of Other-Emptiness* by Tāranātha

(Since Tāranātha's presentation closely follows the views of Döl-b̄o-b̄a Ṡhay-rap-gyel-tsen, illustrative passages from Döl-b̄o-b̄a's *Ocean of Definitive Meaning* are added in clearly marked indents, mostly in the section on the Great Middle Way. Other explanatory material is also added in clearly marked indents.)

*Oṃ svasti.*

Here the entity of the Great Vehicle definitive middle will be identified. It has three parts: a general indication of presentations of tenets, identifying the presentation of the middle, and clearing away extremes imputed by others about the middle.

## I. General Indication of Presentations of Tenets

### *Non-Buddhist Schools of Tenets*

The view and tenets of other schools, the [non-Buddhist] Forders,[a] are devoid of a path of liberation, whereas the view and tenets of our own Buddhist schools are related with a path of liberation. Although the Forders do not have a path of liberation, some do and some do not have doctrines [for achieving] high status[b] [within cyclic existence]. Nihilists,[c] such as the Flung-Afar[d] and so forth, who

---

[a] *mu stegs byed, tīrthakara/ tīrthaṃkara;* etymologically, the term means "those who make a ford to the end," that is, to liberation. The term refers to non-Buddhists.

[b] *mngon par mtho ba, abhyudaya.* These are elevated states, the happinesses, of humans and gods (including demi-gods) relative to animals, hungry ghosts, and hell-beings within the five types of lives in cyclic existence. Since *abhyudaya* is derived from *abhi* + *ud* and Vaman Shivaram Apte's *Sanskrit-English Dictionary* gives as translations "rise (of heavenly bodies), sunrise; rise, prosperity, good fortune, elevation, success" and so forth, *abhyudaya*—both from the viewpoint of meaning and of etymology—means *elevated,* or *high, status* within the realms of cyclic existence. Tibetan and Indian scholars brought the term into Tibetan not as the gloss *bde ba* (happiness) but as *mngon mtho,* literally "manifestly high." I have done the same in English translation through using the term "high status" and "high states."

[c] *med par lta ba can.*

[d] *rgyang 'phen pa, ayata.*

deprecate actions and their effects, and so forth, and who propound harmful actions as the chief doctrine, do not have even a pure path to high status. However, Enumerators,[a] Naked Ones,[b] some followers of a supreme deity, and meditating Forders have a path to high status, because they come to be reborn as humans and gods of the Desire Realm through abandoning ill-deeds and achieving virtues, come to be reborn in the Form Realm through meditatively cultivating the four concentrations, and come to be reborn in the Formless Realm through meditatively cultivating the four formless meditative stabilizations. (See chart, next page.)

The reason why Forders do not have a path of liberation is that they do not abandon this awareness that apprehends the "I" as self, called the "apprehension of a self of persons."[c] For:

- on top of having a steady awareness apprehending the "I" as a self that has continuously come from beginningless cyclic existence, through their tenets they also prove that just that I-self[d] exists with many attributes, meditate on its meaning, and
- they also do not have anything else that is an antidote to this apprehension of self, due to which they cannot abandon the apprehension of self, and
- this apprehension of self is the cause even of all other afflictive emotions.

> Döl-b̄o-b̄a's *Mountain Doctrine* (117): The *Descent into Laṅkā Sūtra* says:
>
> > Mahāmati said, "The matrix-of-One-Gone-Thus taught in other sūtras spoken by the Supramundane Victor was said by the Supramundane Victor to be naturally radiant, pure, and thus from the beginning just pure. The matrix-of-One-Gone-Thus is said to possess the thirty-two marks [of a Buddha] and to exist in the bodies of all sentient beings.

---

a *grangs can pa, sāṃkhya.*

b *gcer bu pa, nirgrantha;* these are the Jainas (*rgyal ba pa*).

c *gang zag gi bdag 'dzin.*

d *nga bdag.*

## *Chart 1: Cyclic Existence: The Three Realms and Nine Levels*

(from the highest levels to the lowest)

III. Formless Realm (*gzugs med khams, ārūpyadhātu*)
- 9. Peak of Cyclic Existence (*srid rtse, bhavāgra*)
- 8. Nothingness (*ci yang med, ākiṃcaya*)
- 7. Limitless Consciousness (*rnam shes mtha' yas, vijñānānantya*)
- 6. Limitless Space (*nam mkha' mtha' yas, ākāśānantya*)

II. Form Realm (*gzugs khams, rūpadhātu*)
- 5. Fourth Concentration (*bsam gtan bzhi pa, caturthadhyāna*)
- 4. Third Concentration (*bsam gtan gsum pa, tritīyadhyāna*)
- 3. Second Concentration (*bsam gtan gnyis pa, dvitīyadhyāna*)
- 2. First Concentration (*bsam gtan dang po, prathamadhyāna*)

I. 1. Desire Realm (*'dod khams, kāmadhātu*)
- (a) Gods of the Desire Realm (*'dod khams kyi lha, kāma-dhātudeva*)
  - Those Who Make Use of Others' Emanations (*gzhan 'phrul dbang byed, paranirmitavaśavartin*)
  - Those Who Enjoy Emanation (*'phrul dga', nirmāṇarati*)
  - Joyous Land (*dga' ldan, tuṣita*)
  - Land Without Combat (*'thab bral, yāma*)
  - Heaven of Thirty-Three (*sum cu rtsa gsum, trayastriṃśa*)
  - Four Great Royal Lineages (*rgyal chen rigs bzhi, cāturma-hārājakāyika*)
- (b) Demi-gods (*lha ma yin, asura*)
- (c) Humans (*mi, manuṣya*)
- (d) Animals (*dud 'gro, tiryañc*)
- (e) Hungry Ghosts (*yi dvags, preta*)
- (f) Hell-beings (*dmyal ba, nāraka*)

"The Supramundane Victor said that like a precious gem wrapped in a dirty cloth, the matrix-of-One-Gone-Thus is wrapped in the cloth of the aggregates, constituents, and sense-spheres, overwhelmed by the force of desire, hatred, and ignorance, and dirtied with the defilements of conceptuality.

"Since this which is dirtied with the defilements of conceptuality was said to be permanent,[a] stable,[b] and everlasting,[c] Supramundane Victor, how is this propounding of a matrix-of-One-Gone-Thus not like the [non-Buddhist] Forders' propounding of a self? Supramundane Victor, the Forders teach and propound a self that is permanent, the agent, without qualities, pervasive, and non-perishing."

The Supramundane Victor said, "Mahāmati, my teaching of a matrix-of-One-Gone-Thus is not like the Forders' propounding of a self. O Mahāmati, the completely perfect Buddhas, Ones-Gone-Thus, Foe Destroyers,[d] teach a matrix-of-One-Gone-Thus for the

---

[a] *rtag pa.*

[b] *brtan pa.*

[c] *ther zug.*

[d] With respect to the translation of *arhant* (*dgra bcom pa*) as "Foe Destroyer," I do this to accord with the usual Tibetan translation of the term and to assist in capturing the flavor of oral and written traditions that frequently refer to this etymology. Arhants have overcome the foe which is the afflictive emotions (*nyon mongs, kleśa*), the chief of which is ignorance.

The Indian and Tibetan translators of Sanskrit and other texts into Tibetan were also aware of the etymology of *arhant* as "worthy one," as they translated the name of the "founder" of the Jaina system, Arhat, as *mchod 'od,* "Worthy of Worship" (see Jam-ȳang-shay-b̄a's *Great Exposition of Tenets, ka* 62a.3). Also, they were aware of Chandrakīrti's gloss of the term as "Worthy One" in his *Clear Words: sadevamānuṣāsurāl lokāt pūnārhatvād arhannityuchyate* (*Mūlamadhyamakakārikās de Nāgārjuna avec la Prasannapadā commentaire de Candrakīrti,* Bibliotheca Buddhica 4 [Osnabrück, Germany: Biblio Verlag, 1970], 486.5), *lha dang mi dang lha ma yin du bcas pa'i 'jig rten gyis mchod par 'os pas dgra bcom pa zhes brjod la* (409.20, Tibetan Cultural Printing Press ed.; also, P5260, vol. 98,

meaning of the words emptiness, limit of reality, nirvāṇa, no production, signlessness, wishlessness, and so forth. So that children might avoid the fear of selflessness, they teach through the means of a matrix-of-One-Gone-Thus the state of non-conceptuality, the object [of wisdom] free from appearances.

"Mahāmati, future and present Bodhisattvas—

---

75.2.2): "Because of being worthy of worship by the world of gods, humans, and demi-gods, they are called Arhants."

Also, they were aware of Haribhadra's twofold etymology in his *Illumination of the Eight Thousand Stanza Perfection of Wisdom Sūtra.* In the context of the list of epithets qualifying the retinue of Buddha at the beginning of the sūtra (see Unrai Wogihara, *Abhisamayālaṃkārālokā Prajñāpāramitā-vyākhyā, The Work of Haribhadra* [Tokyo: Toyo Bunko, 1932-1935; reprint, Tokyo: Sankibo Buddhist Book Store, 1973], 8.18), Haribhadra says:

> They are called *arhant* [Worthy One, from the root *arh* "to be worthy"] since they are worthy of worship, religious donations, and being assembled together in a group, and so forth. (Wogihara, *Abhisamayālaṃkārālokā,* 9.8-9: *sarva evātra pūjā-dakṣiṇā-gaṇa-parikarṣādy-ārhatayarhantaḥ;* P5189, vol. 90, 67.5.7: *'dir thams cad kyang mchod pa dang // yon dang tshogs su 'dub la sogs par 'os pas na dgra bcom pa'o*).

Also:

> They are called *arhant* [Foe Destroyer, *arihan*] because they have destroyed (*hata*) the foe (*ari*). (Wogihara, *Abhisamayālaṃkārālokā,* 10.18: *hatāritvād* ***arhantaḥ;*** P5189, vol. 90, 69.3.6: *dgra rnams bcom pas na dgra bcom pa'o*).

(My thanks to Gareth Sparham for the references to Haribhadra.) Thus, we are dealing with a considered preference in the face of alternative etymologies—"Foe Destroyer" requiring a not unusual *i* infix to make *arihan,* with *ari* meaning "enemy" and *han* meaning "to kill," and thus "Foe Destroyer." Unfortunately, one word in English cannot convey both this meaning and "Worthy of Worship"; thus I have gone with what clearly has become the predominant meaning in Tibet. (For an excellent discussion of the two etymologies of Arhat in Buddhism and Jainism, see L. M. Joshi, *Facets of Jaina Religiousness in Comparative Light,* L.D. Series 85 [Ahmedabad, India: L.D. Institute of Indology, 1981], 53-58.)

great beings—should not adhere to this as a self. Mahāmati, for example, potters make a variety of vessels out of one mass of clay particles with their hands, manual skill, a rod, water, string, and mental dexterity. Mahāmati, similarly the Ones-Gone-Thus also teach the selflessness of phenomena that is an absence of all conceptual signs. Through various [techniques] endowed with wisdom and skill in means—whether they teach it as the matrix-of-One-Gone-Thus or as selflessness—they, like a potter, teach with various formats of words and letters.

"Therefore, Mahāmati, the teaching of the matrix-of-One-Gone-Thus is not like the teaching propounding a self for Forders. Mahāmati, in order to lead Forders who are attached to propounding self, the Ones-Gone-Thus teach the matrix-of-One-Gone-Thus through the teaching of a matrix-of-One-Gone-Thus. Thinking, "How could those with thoughts fallen into incorrect views conceiving of self come to be endowed with thought abiding in the spheres of the three liberations and come to be quickly, manifestly, and completely purified in unsurpassed complete perfect enlightenment?" Mahāmati, for their sake the Ones-Gone-Thus, Foe Destroyers, completely perfect Buddhas, teach the matrix-of-One-Gone-Thus. Consequently, that is not the same as propounding the self of Forders. Therefore, Mahāmati, in order to overcome the view of Forders, they cause them to engage the matrix-of-One-Gone-Thus, selflessness. It is this way: this teaching of the emptiness of phenomena, non-production, non-dualism, and absence of inherent nature is the unsurpassed tenet of Bodhisattvas. Through thoroughly apprehending this teaching of the profound doctrine, one thoroughly apprehends all sūtras of the Great Vehicle."

However, the better Forders have a path to high states,[a] because they also have good views, meditation, and behavior:

- meditation on the coarse impermanence of birth, aging, sickness, and death, and so forth
- knowledge of this lifetime and the Desire Realm as painful
- assertion that gross things such as forms are truthless[b]
- fewer desires and knowing satisfaction
- love and compassion
- the equanimity of meditating on enemies and friends as equal, and so forth
- abandoning the four roots,[c] and so forth.

### *Buddhist Schools of Tenets*

Buddhist schools of tenets are fourfold: Great Exposition School, Sūtra School, Mind-Only School, and Middle Way School. The first two of those are Lesser Vehicle Hearer schools, and the latter two are Great Vehicle schools. With respect to positing them as Lesser Vehicle and Great Vehicle, they are designated this way because of accepting the scriptural collections of the Lesser Vehicle as the finality of Buddha's word and accepting the scriptural collections of the Great Vehicle as the finality of Buddha's word [respectively]. Consequently, these accord with their renown as Lesser Vehicle schools of tenets and Great Vehicle schools of tenets, called "Lesser Vehicle Proponents" and "Great Vehicle Proponents."

However, with respect to positing persons as **persons** of the Lesser Vehicle and **persons** of the Great Vehicle, there is no one-pointed certainty as to school of tenets. For:

- those who have generated attitudes and practices of Great Vehicle paths in their continuums are persons of the Great Vehicle
- those who have generated attitudes and practices of Lesser

---

a *mtho ris.*

b *bden med.*

c Killing, stealing, sexual misconduct, and lying.

Vehicle paths in their continuums are persons of the Lesser Vehicle, and
- if one has not generated any of those two in their continuums, no matter what scriptures one reads and no matter what texts one holds, one is not either a person of the Great Vehicle or a person of the Lesser Vehicle.

Moreover, there are cases of:

- holding Great Vehicle tenets but entering a Lesser Vehicle path
- holding Lesser Vehicle tenets but entering a Great Vehicle path[a]

---

[a] The Ge-luk-b̄a scholar Jam-ȳang-shay-b̄a (*'jam dbyangs bzhad pa ngag dbang brtson grus,* 1648-1722) views this as barely possible (Jeffrey Hopkins, *Maps of the Profound: Jam-yang-shay-ba's Great Exposition of Buddhist and Non-Buddhist Views on the Nature of Reality* [Ithaca, N.Y.: Snow Lion Publications, 2003], 255):

> Except for not negating the bare possibility that there might be Bodhisattvas having the Great Vehicle lineage among the two early Hearer schools, there mainly are only those having the Lesser Vehicle lineage:
> - because the intended trainees of the scriptures of those two schools are necessarily only those having the Lesser Vehicle lineage, and
> - because this is the thought of sūtras and the great chariots [that is, the great scholar-yogis]...
>
> Nāgārjuna's *Precious Garland* (stanza 390) says:
>
> > Bodhisattvas' aspirational wishes, deeds, and dedications [of merit]
> > Were not described in the Hearers' Vehicle.
> > Therefore how could one become
> > A Bodhisattva through it?
>
> Hence, since the two early Hearer schools are not extensive about mainly seeking others' welfare...they do not have the complete mode of sustaining the objects of observation and subjective aspects of the altruistic intention to become enlightened...due to which it is not generated with all of its characteristics. For although there are cases of their wishing to attain Buddhahood, the entanglements of self-cherishing are not

- holding Great Vehicle tenets and entering a Great Vehicle path
- holding Lesser Vehicle tenets and entering a Lesser Vehicle path.

> Jam-ȳang-shay-b̄a's *Great Exposition of Tenets:*[a] Therefore, in accordance with Ke-drup's *Opening the Eyes of the Fortunate:*
>
> - Hearer *persons* must have entered the Hearer path, and even if they not only accept the Great Vehicle scriptural collections but have realized meanings found therein, their strength of attitude [that is, motivation] is small, and hence are involved in their own welfare, as was the case, for instance, with Shāriputra and so forth.
> - Lesser Vehicle *tenet-holders* are those who accept mere enlightenment as well as the path in accordance with the Lesser Vehicle scriptural collections but who do not accept the word of the Great Vehicle or even if they do accept it, do not assert that the meanings expressed therein are uncommon.
>
> Consequently, how could Hearer *persons* and Lesser Vehicle *tenet-holders* be one!

Also, there are a great many who hold tenets but have not entered a path; however, there is not at all a person who has entered the path but does not have tenets.

---

severed, whereby such does not serve as a cause of perfect enlightenment, like, for example, the fact that although a Solitary Realizer's generation of motivation involves a wish to attain Buddhahood, it does not serve as a cause of perfect enlightenment.

[a] Hopkins, *Maps of the Profound,* 194.

## Great Exposition School

From among those [four Buddhist schools of tenets], the Great Exposition School asserts that:

- consciousness—the two, minds and mental factors

  Nga-w̄ang-b̄el-den's *Annotations:*[a] There are forty-six mental factors:

  *FIVE DEFINITE GROUPS*
  - ten mental factors that accompany all main minds: feeling, intention, discrimination, aspiration, contact, intelligence, mindfulness, mental engagement, interest, and stabilization
  - ten virtuous mental factors that accompany all virtuous states: faith, conscientiousness, pliancy, equanimity, shame, embarrassment, non-attachment, non-hatred, non-harmfulness, and effort
  - six great afflictive emotions that accompany all afflicted states: obscuration, non-conscientiousness, laziness, non-faith, lethargy, and excitement
  - two non-virtuous mental factors that accompany all non-virtuous states: non-shame and non-embarrassment
  - ten lesser afflictive emotions: belligerence, resentment, dissimulation, jealousy, verbal spite, concealment, miserliness, deceit, haughtiness, and harmfulness

  *EIGHT MISCELLANEOUS MENTAL FACTORS*
  - desire, anger, pride, doubt, investigation, analysis, sleep, and contrition.

  When five mental factors—forgetfulness, non-introspection, distraction, afflicted view, and non-obscuration—are added to the forty-six mental factors described in Vasubandhu's *Treasury of Manifest Knowledge,* there are the fifty-one mental factors described in Asaṅga's Treatises on the Grounds, Vasubandhu's *Work on the Five Aggregates,*

---

[a] Hopkins, *Maps of the Profound,* 238.

Asaṅga's *Summary of Manifest Knowledge,* and so forth.

- objects—the ten, forms and so forth [that is, visible forms, sounds, odors, tastes, tangible objects, eye sense-power, ear sense-power, nose sense-power, tongue sense-power, and body sense-power]
- non-associated compositional factors[a] such as production and disintegration

Nga-w̄ang-b̄el-den's *Annotations:*[b] There are fourteen non-associated compositional factors:

1. acquisition. This is asserted to be what causes a person to possess virtuous and non-virtuous actions and so forth, like a rope tying up goods. Acquisition of acquisition and so forth are similar.
2. non-acquisition
3. similar lot
4. one having no discrimination
5. absorption without discrimination. This and the next are mindless compositional factors. There are also Proponents of the Great Exposition who assert that these are subtle minds.
6. absorption of cessation
7. life faculty. This is the support of warmth and consciousness.
8. production
9. aging
10. abiding
11. disintegration
12. group of stems. Stems indicate entities.
13. group of words. Words [that is, stems with case endings and so forth] indicate specifics, such as

---

[a] *ldan pa ma yin pa'i 'du byed, viprayuktasaṃskāra.* These are phenomena that are neither form nor consciousness and thus are a separate category; they get their name due to not being associated (*ldan min, viprayukta*) with minds or mental factors.

[b] Hopkins, *Maps of the Profound,* 239.

"compounded phenomena are impermanent."

14. group of letters. Letters are vocalizations that are the bases of setting up stems and words, such as *ka* in *ka dam pa* [a type of tree with fragrant orange blossoms]. In general, *go,* for instance, is a letter, and it is also used as a name for cow, whereby they assert that stems and letters are not mutually exclusive.

- the three uncompounded [phenomena][a]—space and so forth[b]—and
- past and future things[c]

are individually substantially established,[d] and each have factors of true establishment.[e] They assert that gross things and things that are continuums are not truly existent.[f] They say[a] that a

---

a *'dus ma byas, asaṃskṛta.*

b The three renowned uncompounded phenomena are uncompounded space, analytical cessations, and non-analytical cessations. A non-analytical cessation occurs as a result of the incompleteness of the conditions for its production, such as the lack of hunger at the time of intensely concentrating on conversation. Once the moment has passed, the fact that one had no desire for food at that time will never change, and for this reason, its cessation is said to be permanent. An analytical cessation is the state of having eradicated an obstruction such that it will never occur again, as in the case of a complete cessation forever of a particular type of desire through meditation on the four noble truths.

c The past of a thing occurs after its present existence, that is, after its present existence has passed. The future of a thing occurs before its present existence, that is, when its present existence is yet to be.

d *rdzas su grub pa, dravyasiddha.*

e *bden grub, satyasiddha.*

f *bden med.* From Tāranātha's switching between "truly established" and "truly existent" it likely is his position that in the Great Exposition School:

- All phenomena are substantially established and truly established, and individual minute particles and individual moments of consciousnesses are also truly existent (as are uncompounded phenomena).
- However, coarse, or gross, objects such as pots are not truly existent, and continuums such as a stream of consciousness are not truly exis-

consciousness is produced from a truly established object and a truly established sense-power and that an eye [that is, a eye sense-power] actually sees a form.[b]

Among them, those who hold better tenets—the Kashmiri Proponents of the Great Exposition and so forth—assert that all compounded phenomena are impermanent in the sense of disintegrating momentarily and assert that a self of persons, except for being only imputed by an awareness, does not substantially exist. The proponents of worse tenets, such as the Saṃmitīyas and so forth,[c] say that although compounded phenomena are impermanent due to finally disintegrating, they do not disintegrate momentarily.

Gön-chok-jik-may-wang-bo's *Presentation of Tenets:*[d] All

---

tent.

[a] Here, the term "say" (*zer*) implies that neither of these assertions is true. In the system of the Great Middle Way consciousnesses (*rnam shes*), as well as all impermanent phenomena, are necessarily not truly established, whereas self-arisen pristine wisdom (*rang byung ye shes*) necessarily is truly established.

[b] Unlike the other schools, the Great Exposition School claims that not just an eye sense consciousness but also an eye sense power, which is composed of subtle matter, sees a visible form such as a color or a shape. As Gön-chok-jik-may-wang-bo's *Presentation of Tenets* says:

> They assert that even a physical eye sense power that is the base [of an eye consciousness] perceives form, for they say that if a consciousness alone were the seer, then one would see forms that are obstructed by walls and so forth.

A consciousness, being formless, is not obstructed by form; however, because the support of an eye consciousness is a physical sense power, the seer also incorporates form and so is obstructed by form. See Geshe Lhundup Sopa and Jeffrey Hopkins, *Cutting through Appearances: The Practice and Theory of Tibetan Buddhism* (Ithaca, N.Y.: Snow Lion Publications, 1989), 199.

[c] Some scholars speak of "five Saṃmitīya schools"—Vatsīputrīyas, Bhadrayānīyas, Kurukullas, Dharmaguptakas, and Uttarīyas. See Hopkins, *Maps of the Profound,* 220-222.

[d] Sopa and Hopkins, *Cutting through Appearances,* 194-196. Gön-

> compounded phenomena are necessarily impermanent but do not necessarily disintegrate moment by moment, for the Proponents of the Great Exposition assert that following production there is the activity of duration, and then the activity of disintegration occurs.[a]

Therefore, they assert all sorts of effective things that are

---

chok-jik-may-w̄ang-b̄o identifies the Proponents of the Great Exposition in general as asserting that the activities of production, duration, and disintegration occur serially, whereas Tāranātha identifies only the "Saṃmitīyas and so forth" as asserting this. For more discussion of the characteristics of compounded phenomena in the Great Exposition School and Sūtra School, see Hopkins, *Maps of the Profound,* 240-242.

[a] Sopa and Hopkins (*Cutting through Appearances,* 195-196) comment:

> All Buddhist schools agree that coarse impermanence is the production of a thing such as a table, its lasting for a period of time, and finally its disintegration such as its being consumed by fire. Buddhist schools also assert a subtle impermanence that, except for developed yogis, is not accessible to direct experience. For example, death, which is an instance of coarse impermanence, is commonly experienced, but the momentary aging of a person, which is a subtle impermanence, is not.
>
> The Proponents of the Great Exposition differ from the other Buddhist schools in asserting that the factors of production, abiding, aging, and disintegration are external to the entity that undergoes these. All other systems hold that production itself is a cause or sufficient condition for disintegration; disintegration begins *with,* and not *after,* the very first moment of production. In all systems except the Great Exposition School, that which is produced is that which abides and that which disintegrates. This is because production is understood to be the arising of a new entity due to certain causes; abiding is the continued existence of that type of entity; disintegration is its quality of not lasting a second moment; and aging is the factor of its being a different entity from the entity of the previous moment. In this way, the four can occur simultaneously. The Great Exposition School, however, asserts that the factors of production, duration, aging, and disintegration act on the object and occur in series, one after the other.

continuums.[a] They assert that, although a permanent, unitary, and self-powered I-self as is imputed by the [non-Buddhist] Forders does not exist, in general the mere I-self is substantially established and truly established.

> Ḡön-chok-jik-may-w̄ang-b̄o's *Presentation of Tenets:*[b] From among the eighteen subschools of the Great Exposition School, the five Saṃmitīya subschools do not assert that a person's emptiness of being substantially existent in the sense of being self-sufficient is the subtle selflessness because they consider that a substantially existent or self-sufficient person exists.

> Ḡön-chok-jik-may-w̄ang-b̄o's *Presentation of Tenets:*[c]
>
> *Objection:* In that case, the Vātsīputrīya [a subschool of the Great Exposition School] would not be proponents of Buddhist tenets because they assert a self of persons.
>
> *Answer:* There is no such fallacy because the self that they assert is a self-sufficient, substantially existent self whereas the selflessness of the four seals refers to the absence of a permanent, unitary, independent self and that [selflessness] is asserted even by the five Saṃmitīyas schools [—the Vātsīputrīyas being one of the five—although they do assert an inexpressible self].[d]

---

a *rgyun gyi dngos po yang ci rigs par 'dod.* The significance of this assertion appears to be that since impermanence takes place over a series of moments of production, abiding, and disintegration, most effective things have to be continuums rather than merely momentary.

b Sopa and Hopkins, *Cutting through Appearances,* 204.

c Ibid., 177.

d Sopa and Hopkins (*Cutting through Appearances,* 177-178) comment:

> In his *Great Exposition of Tenets* [Hopkins, *Maps of the Profound,* 219-222] Jam-ȳang-shay-b̄a, who is identified as Ḡön-chok-jik-may-w̄ang-b̄o's previous incarnation, does not accept that the Vātsīputrīyas assert a self-sufficient, substantially existent person because they, like the other Proponents of a Person (*gang zag smra ba, pudgalavādin*), hold that the person is inexpressible as either substantially existent or imputedly existent, or as the same

Even if they not do actually have a path of liberation due to the fallacy of a view of self, they go for refuge to the Three Jewels and have ethics motivated by a wish for liberation as well as the three—hearing, thinking, and meditating—whereby they gradually come to have the fortune of attaining liberation.

The Proponents of the Great Exposition assert that the Seven Sections of Manifest Knowledge are the word of Buddha.

> Gön-chok-jik-may-wang-bo's *Presentation of Tenets:*[a] The Proponents of the Great Exposition assert that the Seven Sections of Manifest Knowledge were spoken by Buddha [and written down by Foe Destroyers].

However, they say that many within the Sets of Sūtras have a thought behind them[b] and require interpretation.

---

as or different from the aggregates, whereas a self-sufficient, substantially existent person is necessarily able to stand by itself separate from the aggregates. Thus, although Gön-chok-jik-may-wang-bo agrees with Jam-yang-shay-ba that the selflessness mentioned in the four seals refers to "the absence of a permanent, unitary, independent self," he does not agree with Jam-yang-shay-ba's position that the Vātsīputrīyas do not assert a substantially existent person. In holding that the Vātsīputrīyas assert a substantially existent person, Gön-chok-jik-may-wang-bo is probably following his teacher, Jang-gya Röl-bay-dor-jay, who, in his *Presentations of Tenets* (77.5-84.12), gives a long refutation of Jam-yang-shay-ba on this topic. However, Gön-chok-jik-may-wang-bo does not accept Jang-gya's conclusion (84.4) that the Vātsīputrīyas, though Buddhist, are not actual proponents of Buddhist tenets. Gön-chok-jik-may-wang-bo maintains that they are actual proponents of Buddhist tenets by holding...that the selflessness indicated in the four seals refers to "the absence of a permanent, unitary, independent self." In this way, Gön-chok-jik-may-wang-bo does not agree completely either with his previous incarnation, Jam-yang-shay-ba, or with his teacher Jang-gya.

a Sopa and Hopkins, *Cutting through Appearances,* 215.

b *dgongs pa can.*

Jam-ȳang-shay-b̄a's *Great Exposition of Tenets:*[a] Certain Proponents of the Great Exposition assert, in accordance with the description in Bhāvaviveka's *Blaze of Reasoning,* that all of [Buddha's] word is just of definitive meaning [that is, literal] and do not assert that there are interpretable meanings. In addition, there are also [some] who assert that there are both definitive meanings and meanings requiring interpretation. Not only that, but also all later Proponents of the Great Exposition and even the Vatsīputrīyas assert that even Perfection of Wisdom Sūtras require interpretation, saying that:

- The statements that non-production and the absence of true existence refer to the type of production and truth imputed by Forders such as the Sāṃkhyas and so forth.
- Likewise, the statements of the non-existence of nature, the non-existence of attainment, abandonment, and so forth and the non-existence of things also are in consideration that the nature and so forth and permanent effective things as imputed by Forders do not exist.[b]

Consequently, they assert that views and practices must be asserted in accordance with the system found in the "treatise"; that treatise, furthermore, is identified as [Vasumitra's] *Exposition of Particulars.*[c]

---

a Hopkins, *Maps of the Profound,* 235.

b *drang don, neyārtha.* Ḡön-chok-jik-may-w̄ang-b̄o holds, to the contrary, that in the Great Exposition School, "Buddha's word is always literal." Again, Ḡön-chok-jik-may-w̄ang-b̄o is in disagreement with his previous incarnation, Jam-ȳang-shay-b̄a, who, like Tāranātha, cogently holds that only *some* Proponents of the Great Exposition hold that Buddha's word is always literal, for other subschools of the Great Exposition hold that there are both definitive and interpretable passages among Buddha's word.

c *bye brag bshad pa.* This is the *mahāvibhāṣā, bye brag bshad mtsho* [or *mdzod*] *chen mo* (*Great Ocean* or *Treasury of Exposition of Particulars*). It was translated into Tibetan from the Chinese (Taisho 1545) by the

## Sūtra School

The Proponents of the Sūtra School[a] assert that from among the aforementioned phenomena:

- Uncompounded [phenomena] and non-associated compositional factors are "imputedly existent,"[b] that is, only imputed by an awareness and hence do not truly exist.

  Jam-ȳang-shay-b̄a's *Great Exposition of Tenets:*[c] Uncompounded phenomena must be neither substantially existent nor substantially established because:

  - a mere negative of obstructive contact is posited as "space"; non-production due to incompleteness of conditions is posited as a "non-analytical cessation"; and a mere state of having separated from any [level of] afflictive emotions through the wisdom of individual investigation is posited as an "analytical cessation,"
  - their entities are not demonstrable separately as "It is this," the way forms and feelings are,
  - and their functions also are not demonstrable separately as "It does such-and-such," the way eyes and so forth are...

- Among forms and so forth gross objects and continuums[d] are not truly established, and among consciousnesses continuums

---

Chinese monk-scholar Fa Zun (aka *blo bzang chos 'phags*) only in 1949 but is, as yet, unpublished. Because they hold that their tenets must be asserted in accordance with the *Exposition of Particulars,* they are called Proponents of the Great Exposition.

[a] Tāranātha does not make a division of the Sūtra School into a Sūtra School Following Scripture and a Sūtra School Following Reasoning, as Ge-luk-b̄a scholars uniquely do. His presentation of the Sūtra School is more like Ge-luk-b̄a presentations of the Sūtra School Following Scripture.

[b] *btags yod, prajñaptisat.*

[c] Hopkins, *Maps of the Profound,* 271.

[d] *rags rgyun.*

are not truly established.

- Past and future phenomena also are only imputedly existent.[a]
- Only present minute particles and only present moments of consciousness are partless and truly established.
- An eye [that is, an eye sense-power] does not see forms.

> Jam-ȳang-shay-b̄a's *Great Exposition of Tenets:*[b] Physical sense powers are not fit to be valid cognitions because of being matter and because of not being able to comprehend their objects and because of being empty of luminosity and knowing...
>
> *Objection:* If consciousness [alone] is what sees, then it would see even what is obstructed by a wall and so forth.
>
> *Answer:* That is not so because an eye consciousness is not produced with respect to what is obstructed and, not being produced, it does not apprehend an object.
>
> *Question:* Are eye consciousnesses not produced with respect to anything obstructed or intervened?
>
> *Answer:* There is no certainty; despite intervention by a glass vessel, mica, a crystal, or water, [objects] are seen. Therefore, even the statement by you Proponents of the Great Exposition that [an eye consciousness] does not see what is intervened is uncertain. For an eye consciousness is produced with respect to whatever form has no obstacle to its appearing even while it is obstructed, and an eye consciousness is not produced with respect to what has an obstacle to its appearing.

- Even an eye consciousness does not explicitly see forms.[c] That

---

[a] Ḡön-chok-jik-may-w̄ang-b̄o says that past and future phenomena are permanent.

[b] Hopkins, *Maps of the Profound,* 271.

[c] *gzugs dngos su mi mthong.* Jam-ȳang-shay-b̄a (Hopkins, *Maps of the Profound,* 275-276) criticizes a similar view that the Sūtra School holds that an eye consciousness, for instance, does not directly perceive its object:

> Chandrakīrti's autocommentary on his *Supplement* explains that comprehension of an aspect similar to [the object] is imputed

which is seen by an eye consciousness is a dawning of an appearance of a form, which is consciousness in an aspect of form [or representation of form]. However, for that aspect to dawn, there is an external object, a visible form and so forth, that casts an aspect [of itself to the consciousness].

Jam-ȳang-shay-b̄a's *Great Exposition of Tenets*:[a] The position of the Proponents of the Great Exposition is that:

> An unaspected sense awareness
> Directly knows aggregations of particles.

In order to refute this, Proponents of Sūtra and above...say:

> It is not suitable to know objects that illumine themselves without aspect [that is, without the medium of a representation] because those objects are not entities illuminating themselves and because if objects were luminous, then just as blue [being blue does not depend on a consciousness apprehending it], those objects would be illuminated even without depending on consciousness. Therefore, that which luminously perceives a present object is consciousness.

Proponents of Sūtra assert that the minute particles that are the basis of an appearance as blue, long, and so forth exist as external particles. The distinguishing feature of the Proponents of Mind-Only and the Proponents of the Middle who assert an emptiness of duality [of subject and object] is that there are no external particles that are the

---

with the convention of comprehending it.

About this, it follows that many earlier Tibetans saying that the Proponents of Sūtra assert that the [external] object is obscure (*don lkog na mo*) is not feasible because the Proponents of Sūtra also assert that an eye consciousness directly sees form (*gzugs mngon sum du mthong ba*), since they assert that an eye consciousness clearly perceives [its object] by way of having [been generated in its] aspect.

[a] Hopkins, *Maps of the Profound*, 274-275.

basis of appearance.

All of our own proponents of [consciousness as] having aspects [that is, the Sūtra School and above] assert that it is like the fact that when a person looks at a clear piece of glass the far side of which has been painted, both the glass and the paint are similar in being seen, but the glass is realized from its own entity and the color is realized in the manner of an image. [About the Proponents of Sūtra] the master Bodhibhadra says:

> When a person looks at a glass the color of which has been affected by shell-paint, the eye apprehends both glass and paint; the glass is apprehended directly and the paint is apprehended in the manner of an image, whereby the person apprehends two apprehended objects. These Proponents of Sūtra propound that accordingly:
>
> - that which is perceived directly is an aspect of only consciousness
> - the basis of the consciousness' appearing as color and shape is a separate collection of minute particles
> - the consciousness is [generated into having the aspect of] those entities without contacting them [directly]
>
> whereby there are two apprehended objects.

- The Seven Sections of Manifest Knowledge and so forth are not the word of Buddha.

> Jam-ȳang-shay-b̄a's *Great Exposition of Tenets:*[a] Certain Proponents of Sūtra say that the Seven Sections are not the word [of Buddha] because they were composed by seven Foe Destroyers such as Shāriputra and so forth...For most Proponents of Sūtra, not only are the Seven Sections not the word [of Buddha], they are not even the word of Foe

---

[a] Ibid., 268.

Destroyers because [those treatises] propound that space is a permanent substance, and so forth, and Superiors would not assert such, since they are fully empowered as persons who have valid cognition with respect to [understanding] phenomena. [These treatises] were composed by ordinary beings having the same names [as For Destroyers]...

*Question:* If the Seven Sections are not [the scriptural division of] manifest knowledge, then because [the scriptural division of] manifest knowledge is not to be observed [anywhere else], it would not be feasible for the Supramundane Victor to speak of "the three scriptural divisions."

*Answer:* Although it is true that [the scriptural division of] manifest knowledge is not separate, there is no fallacy of unsuitable non-existence of three scriptural divisions, since the scriptural division of manifest knowledge is the descriptions of the specific and general characters of phenomena here and there in the sets of discourses and the discipline.

- Since treatises, such as [Vasumitra's] *Exposition of Particulars,* contain mistakes, tenets must be [delineated] in concert with the Sets of Sūtras.[a]

Both of these schools of proponents of tenets [that is, the Great Exposition School and the Sūtra School] also say that the word of Buddha is just these scriptural collections spoken for the sake of Hearers and that all these renowned as Great Vehicle sūtras, such as the Perfection of Wisdom Sūtras, the *Pile of Jewels Sūtra,* the *Buddhāvataṃsaka Sūtra,* and so forth are not the word of the Conqueror [Buddha].[b]

---

[a] This explains why they are called Proponents of Sūtra (*mdo sde pa, sautrāntika*).

[b] Jam-ȳang-shay-b̄a's position (Hopkins, *Maps of the Profound,* 268-269) is different:

> Even most Proponents of Sūtra Following Scripture and Proponents of Sūtra Following Reasoning assert that the Great Vehicle scriptural collections are the Word [of Buddha] requiring

Nga-w̄ang-b̄el-den's *Annotations:*[a] [Earlier members of Hearer schools say:]

- It follows that the subject, the Great Vehicle scriptural collections, were not spoken by Buddha because of not being included in the three scriptural collections and because of teaching other paths such as attaining purification and release through bathing, fasting, and repeating mantra, as is the case, for example, with the Vedāntins...
- It follows that the subject, the Great Vehicle scriptural collections, were not spoken by Buddha because of deprecating—as not truly existent—all, that is to say, actions and their effects, the four truths, the Three Jewels, and so forth, as is the case, for example, with the Ayatas...
- It follows that the subject, the Great Vehicle scriptural collections, were not spoken by Buddha because of not being included in the texts of the eighteen [Hearer] schools, as is the case, for example, with the opinions

---

interpretation...According to some Proponents of Sūtra such as Saṅghagupta there is a thought behind the words of the Perfection of Wisdom Sūtras and so forth saying, "All phenomena do not exist, do not exist," because it would be unsuitable for the meaning of the statement that "phenomena do not exist" to be that phenomena utterly do not exist, and, therefore, scripture and reasoning establish that the meaning is to be taken as referring to the lowliness and smallness of [impermanent] objects...With respect to the statements in the Perfection of Wisdom Sūtras [that all phenomena] are nothings and so forth, since effective things are momentary, they are said to be nothings and so forth, these being terms of lowliness...Also, since non-things are plentiful and effective things are fewer, [all phenomena] are called "non-things." And they are called natureless, unproduced, unceased, and so forth because of not being produced beforehand and passing away afterwards, as, for example, when someone with little wealth is said to have no wealth.

[a] Hopkins, *Maps of the Profound,* 195-196.

of the Vedāntins...

- It follows that the subject, the Great Vehicle scriptural collections, are not included within those eighteen,

  1. because of not being gathered on the occasion of the first gathering together of [Buddha's] word, and
  2. because even if they came to be distinguished later, they were not included by those making the second gathering together of [Buddha's] word, and so forth, and
  3. because of contradicting the statement that all products are impermanent by teaching that a One-Gone-Thus is permanent, and
  4. because of contradicting the statement that all phenomena are selfless by teaching a pervasive matrix of One-Gone-Thus and a consciousness that takes [rebirth, that is, a mind-basis-of-all], and
  5. because of contradicting the statement that nirvāṇa is peace by teaching that a Buddha does not pass beyond sorrow [that is, pass into nirvāṇa, or die], and
  6. because they prophesy [Buddha-enlightenment for] Hearers, and
  7. because they intensely deride Foe Destroyers, and
  8. because they teach that it is suitable to pay obeisance to householders, and
  9. because they praise Bodhisattvas as surpassing Ones-Gone-Thus, and
  10. because the prayers of Bodhisattvas such as for the sky-treasury are only words, and
  11. because the entire teaching becomes twisted by their propounding that Shākyamuni is an emanation [of a being who attained enlightenment much earlier], and
  12. because it is not correct that [a Buddha] is always in meditative equipoise, and
  13. because many [Great Vehicle] sūtras set forth

fruitless praises [of its practices], and
14. because they teach that actions have no effects by propounding that even very great ill-deeds are destroyed from the root, and
15. because other Very Vast Sūtras were taught, and
16. because they are not indicated among the divisions [of the Buddhist schools to come in the future as depicted] in [King] Kṛkṛ's dream.

Therefore, this Great Vehicle was not set forth by the Buddha. It is definite that devils composed many various things to deceive beings of bad intelligence and fools.

They say that the Great Vehicle and Lesser Vehicle differ in terms of the activities of persons but there are not different scriptures.[a]

All of their assertions of true establishment and their refutations of the Great Vehicle are faults of mistaken tenets.[b] Others—such as the selflessness of persons, momentary impermanence, and so forth—are unmistaken in themselves.

Nga-w̄ang-b̄el-den's *Annotations:*[c]

*Proponent of the Great Exposition:* Although whatever is a compounded thing is necessarily impermanent, it is non-momentary.

*Proponent of Sūtra:* It follows that things made upon the collection and aggregation of causes and conditions are momentary because they last only for the moment of production. Compounded phenomena such as forms and so forth are seen to be included among what disintegrate, and

---

a According to the Great Exposition School and Sūtra School, Great Vehicle practitioners are those few who, like Shākyamuni, seek Buddhahood in order to be of greater service to others, whereas Hearers and Solitary Realizers seek mainly to escape cyclic existence for themselves.

b In the Great Middle Way no impermanent phenomena are truly established.

c Hopkins, *Maps of the Profound,* 265-266. Nga-w̄ang-b̄el-den is contrasting the Sūtra School's view of momentary impermanence in the sense of just existing for a moment, with the assertion in the Great Exposition School that impermanence occurs over a series of moments.

the entity due to which forms and so forth finally disintegrate exists from the very production of those compounded phenomena; hence, they disintegrate immediately after being produced. Therefore, it is clear that forms and so forth are momentary.

*Proponent of the Great Exposition:* The entity of production is one entity, and the entity of final disintegration another.

*Proponent of Sūtra:* That cannot be said because there are the faults that:

- If these two entities are not different from the thing [for example, a form], it [absurdly] follows that [the two entities themselves] are not different.
- If the thing [for example, a form] is not different from these two entities, it follows that [the two entities are not (?)] different.

The first consequence contradicts your own assertion [that the two entities are different]. If the second is accepted, [then your assertion that things] are not momentary falls apart.

*Proponent of the Great Exposition:* Mountains and so forth, which abide for a while, are produced by their own causes as having the nature of abiding temporarily.

*Proponent of Sūtra:* Just that very nature that they have at the time of production is just what they have at the end; hence, mountains and so forth never would not remain. Therefore, if something is produced as having a nature of abiding in the second moment, just as at the time of the first moment it has the nature of abiding for two moments, so at the time of the second moment it also would necessarily have the nature of abiding for two moments. Hence, it would never disintegrate.

*Proponent of the Great Exposition:* Due to the fact that mountains and so forth are produced by their causes as having a steady nature, they indeed would not change into other entities even in the end, but another cause that makes them cease causes them to disintegrate.

*Proponent of Sūtra:* It is not reasonable [to say that something produced as having a steady nature is later made to disintegrate by another cause]:

- because something that has the nature of non-disintegration would not disintegrate when a cause of disintegration approaches, and
- because to say, "Although it does not have an inner nature of disintegration, it will disintegrate due to such and such" is a contradiction of your own words, like saying, "Although Devadatta has the quality of not dying, he will die."

*Proponent of the Great Exposition:* Although initially it does not have an inner nature of disintegration, when a cause of cessation approaches it is generated into an entity possessing an inner nature of disintegration.

*Proponent of Sūtra:* When a cause of cessation approaches, the prior nature of non-disintegration either continues or does not continue. If it continues, the contradiction would accrue of saying that it is both non-disintegrative and disintegrative. If it does not continue, then because the production and cessation of the two—the nature and that which has the nature—are not different, the former thing [which has the nature] also would not exist; thus what would be generated into having an inner nature of disintegration? For, there would be no basis to be generated into having an inner nature of disintegration, just as it is not suitable for a flower in the sky to be generated into having an inner nature of disintegration.

Therefore, since it is not suitable for something that does not have an inner nature of disintegration to disintegrate, and products such as forms are also seen to disintegrate, they are produced by their own causes into just having an inner nature of disintegration. For this reason they necessarily disintegrate immediately after their production, whereby they are established as momentary...

*Proponent of the Great Exposition:* The temporary abiding of mountains and so forth is produced by causes.

*Proponent of Sūtra:* It [absurdly] follows that they would never fail to abide because in just the way they are produced by causes, so they would also be just that way in the end.

## Mind-Only School

The Proponents of Mind-Only assert that external objects are cases of consciousness itself appearing as this and that, like dream-forms and so forth.

Jam-ȳang-shay-b̄a's *Great Exposition of Tenets:*[a] With respect to the teaching of other-powered natures by way of eight examples, they are taught as being like:

- [a magician's] illusions in order to overcome the doubt wondering how one could observe objects
- mirages in order to overcome doubt wondering how minds and mental factors arise without external objects
- dreams in order to overcome doubt wondering how, if there are no external objects, one gets involved in activities of desire and non-desire
- reflections in order to overcome doubt wondering how, if there are no external objects, one could accomplish the wanted effects of virtuous actions and the unwanted effects of non-virtuous actions
- hallucinations in order to overcome doubt wondering how, if there are no external objects, the varieties of consciousness arise
- echoes in order to overcome doubt wondering how, if there are no external objects, the varieties of expressions arise
- a moon [reflected in] water in order to overcome doubt wondering how, if there are no external objects, the objects of activities of correct meditative stabilization arise
- emanations in order to overcome doubt wondering

[a] Hopkins, *Maps of the Profound,* 341.

> how, if there are no external objects, Bodhisattvas are born in accordance with their thought [to accomplish the aims of sentient beings].[a]

What appear this way do not exist externally. For example, to illustrate this with a form:

> What is renowned to be an eye sense-power is the mind appearing in the aspect of an eye; therefore, legitimately qualified[b] eyes do not exist. Also, what is renowned as a form is the mind appearing in the aspect of a form; legitimately qualified forms do not exist. Therefore, it merely seems that an eye consciousness is produced from those [that is, from an eye sense-power and a form]. Hence, the appearance of even all three of these as different is mistaken, and they are of the same substance in the entity of consciousness.[c] Consequently, an eye consciousness' seeing a form is its seeing itself, and the establishment of a form that (1) casts its aspect [to a consciousness] from the outside—other than consciousness—and (2) is a cause of the dawning of the aspect of a form [in a consciousness] does not at all exist. However, they assert that in the perspective of non-investigation and non-analysis, "The eye sees a form," and so forth, but when analyzed, form is not established, and a consciousness that appears as a form is truly established.

---

a For the passage in Asaṅga's *Summary of the Great Vehicle* on which this list of eight examples is based, see Jeffrey Hopkins, *Reflections on Reality: The Three Natures and Non-Natures in the Mind-Only School* (Berkeley: University of California Press, 2002), 438-439; P5549, vol. 112, 224.5.5-225.1.4; Étienne Lamotte, *La Somme du grand véhicule d'Asaṅga*, reprint, 2 vols., Publications de l'Institute Orientaliste de Louvain 8 (Louvain: Université de Louvain, 1973), vol. 1, 38-39 (II.27), and vol. 2, 122-124; and John P. Keenan, *The Summary of the Great Vehicle by Bodhisattva Asaṅga: Translated from the Chinese of Paramārtha* (Berkeley, Calif.: Numata Center for Buddhist Translation and Research, 1992), 52-53.

b *rang mtshan pa.*

c *shes pa'i ngo bor rdzas gcig pa.*

Therefore, they assert that:

> The entities of all consciousnesses, such as a main consciousness[a] and so forth, are truly established, but the two—the apprehended factor, which is the appearance of an object as existing externally, and an apprehending factor, which is the appearance of a knower as existing internally—are mistakes. Hence, the two, apprehended-object and apprehending-subject, do not exist, but consciousness devoid of the two, apprehended-object and apprehending-subject, is truly established.

Consequently, they assert that since an apprehended-factor and an apprehending-factor are not established as different, this serves as the non-duality of apprehended-object and apprehending-subject, and the mere entity of consciousness[b] is pristine wisdom.

Although, in their own system, the Proponents of Mind-Only claim that they refute apprehended-object and apprehending-subject, in the consideration of higher schools of tenets they have not come to refute apprehended-object and apprehending-subject because although they assert a mere non-difference of substantial entity of apprehended-object and apprehending-subject, they have come to assert that an apprehending-subject exists from its own side.[c]

> Döl-b̄o-b̄a's *Mountain Doctrine* (251): Kalkī Puṇḍarīka's *Stainless Light* says, "Now let us set forth the yogic practitioners' fallacy of an apprehending subject: Those who propound that all three existences are just consciousness assert consciousness," and, "Even the yogic practitioners have an apprehender that is consciousness,"...If an apprehender exists, it is not fitting to be devoid of a self of phenomena.

Thus, mistaken are their assertions that:

---

a *rnam shes.*

b *rnam shes kyi rang ngo tsam.*

c *'dzin pa rang ngos nas yod pa.*

- Cognitionals[a] that appear as external objects such as forms are truly established.
- The mere entity of consciousness in isolation[b] is the pristine wisdom of non-duality of apprehended-object and apprehending-subject.[c]
- The entity of an apprehending-subject is not consciousness itself but is the mere factor that appears differently from the cognition appearing as an object.[d]

Their other [assertions] are non-erroneous.

## Middle Way School

The Middle Way School is of two types: Ordinary Middle Way[e] and Great Middle Way.[f]

### *Ordinary Middle Way School*

In the country of Tibet, the Ordinary Middle Way is renowned as self-emptiness,[g] and in both India and Tibet [this school] is renowned as the Proponents of Non-Nature.[h] This is the system of the masters Buddhapālita, Bhāvaviveka, Vimuktasena, and Shāntarakṣhita, as well as their followers.[i]

---

a *rnam rig, vijñapti.*

b *rnam shes kyi ngo ldog tsam;* this is an abbreviation of *rnam shes kyi ngo bo'i ldog pa tsam,* the mere entity-isolate of consciousness.

c Reading ***gzung*** *'dzin* for ***gzugs*** *'dzin* (497.7 and 178.2).

d In the Great Middle Way pristine wisdom (*ye shes*) is permanent, truly established, and an ultimate that is entirely separate from consciousness (*rnam shes*), which is impermanent, not truly established, conventional, and bound in ignorance. Since an apprehending-subject is merely a mistake, consciousness itself (or the mere entity of consciousness) is merely a mistake and cannot be pristine wisdom.

e *dbu ma phal pa.*

f *dbu ma chen po.*

g *rang stong.*

h *ngo bo nyid med par smra ba, niḥsvabhāvavādin.*

i Tāranātha holds that all of these scholars are actually Proponents of

Although among them there are many different divisions with respect to tenets, they all agree in asserting that:

- All these phenomena—all compounded things (that is, the two, forms and minds, as well as non-associated compositional factors) and all uncompounded phenomena and non-things, such as space—are conventionalities.[a]
- The mere absence of true existence, which is their nature, is the ultimate.[b]
- Those two [that is, conventional truths[c] and ultimate truths[d]] are inexpressible as either one entity or different entities[e] and merely differ in the presentation of them. Since nothing at all exists in the entity of the ultimate basic element,[f] the voidness of proliferations[g] is taught through the example of space. Through the example of a magician's illusions, it is taught that although when conventionalities appear, they are empty of truth, their appearance is unimpeded.
- Both of these [that is, conventional truths and ultimate truths] are beyond all proliferations, such as existence and non-existence, is and is not, and so forth.

---

the Great Middle Way, for as he says below (p. 92), "That Bhāvaviveka, Buddhapālita, and so forth are renowned as Proponents of Self-Emptiness and Proponents of Non-Nature is a case of mainly taking what is renowned to the ordinary world." In *Mountain Doctrine* Döl-b̄o-b̄a cites these scholars (except for Shāntarakṣhita, whom he does not cite at all) in the context of the Great Middle Way. For Buddhapālita, see *Mountain Doctrine*, 343 and 530; Bhāvaviveka or Bhāvaviveka the Lesser (*legs ldan chung ba*), 307 and 469; Vimuktasena, 428.

[a] *kun rdzob.*

[b] *don dam.*

[c] *kun rdzob bden pa, saṃvṛtisatya.*

[d] *don dam bden pa, paramārthasatya.*

[e] Ge-luk-b̄a scholars uniformly assert that the two truths are one entity and different isolates (*ngo bo gcig la ldog pa tha dad*); for instance, see Jam-ȳang-shay-b̄a's presentation in Hopkins, *Maps of the Profound*, 896ff.

[f] *don dam dbyings.*

[g] *spros bral.*

Moreover, this system of tenets is mistaken in:[a]

- asserting that the ultimate noumenon[b] is like space, a mere negation of proliferations[c]

  Döl-b̄o-b̄a's *Mountain Doctrine* (118): Because the uncompounded noumenon transcends the momentary, it is permanent, stable, and everlasting. It is not that it, like space, is without any of the qualities, powers, and aspects of a Buddha, and it is not like the self of persons that [non-Buddhist] Forders impute to be permanent.

  Döl-b̄o-b̄a's *Mountain Doctrine* (470): Similarly, those who assert that in the mode of subsistence, except for exclusions and non-affirming negatives, there are not at all any inclusions, positives, and affirming negatives are extremely mistaken because I have repeatedly explained and will explain that:

  - Natural exclusion, negation, and abandonment are complete in the mode of subsistence, since all flaws are naturally non-existent and non-established in the mode of subsistence.
  - Natural realizations of the inclusionary, the positive, and affirming negatives are primordially complete [in the mode of subsistence], since all noumenal qualities are naturally complete in their basis.[d]

- saying that a Buddha's pristine wisdom and so forth are

---

a The first three of these are asserted in Ge-luk-b̄a presentations.

b *don dam chos nyid.*

c *spros pa bkag tsam.* According to the Ordinary Middle Way School, just as space is a mere negation of obstructive contact, so the ultimate noumenon is a mere negation of the proliferations of true existence. In the Great Middle Way, however, the ultimate noumenon is an affirming negative, not a mere absence or non-affirming negative, and includes positives, since ultimate Buddha-qualities of body, speech, and mind are integrally contained in the ultimate.

d See also Döl-b̄o-b̄a's citation of Aṅgulimāla's criticism of the position that "The Buddha is like space," in *Mountain Doctrine,* 210-213.

conventionalities and do not truly exist[a]

> Döl-b̄o-b̄a's *Mountain Doctrine* (329): Whereas the partless, omnipresent pristine wisdom of the element of attributes[b] always abides pervading all, the extreme of non-existence is the deprecation that it does not exist and is not established and is empty of its own entity.

- asserting that even ultimate truth does not truly exist[c]

> Döl-b̄o-b̄a's *Mountain Doctrine* (342):
>
> *Objection:* Since truth does not exist in any phenomenon, the ultimately true does not occur.
>
> *Answer:* That is not so. If something is not true conventionally, it is not suitable as a conventional truth, and hence that which is a conventional truth is conventionally true and is not ultimately true. Just so, if something is not ultimately true, it is not suitable as an ultimate truth, and hence that which is an ultimate truth is ultimately true and is not conventionally true.

and in particular, mistaken also is the Consequentialists'[d] non-assertion of anything—this being in order to avoid others' debates—despite positing a presentation of tenets.

> D̄zong-ka-b̄a's *Great Exposition of the Stages of the Path:*[e] Nowadays some who wish to be Middle Way Consequentialists [say]:

---

[a] In Ge-luk-b̄a presentations all types of mind, including a Buddha's pristine wisdom, are impermanent, even though at Buddhahood pristine wisdom is uninterruptedly continual. In the Great Middle Way, however, pristine wisdom itself is ultimate and, therefore, permanent and truly existent.

[b] *chos kyi dbyings, dharmadhātu.*

[c] In the Great Middle Way, ultimate truth itself ultimately exists and is truly established.

[d] *thal 'gyur pa rnams, prāsaṅgikāḥ.*

[e] Hopkins, *Meditation on Emptiness,* 549-550; also Elizabeth Napper, *Dependent-Arising and Emptiness* (London: Wisdom Publications, 1989), 116ff.

Our own system even conventionally does not have any assertions based on the ultimate or the conventional. For if we had such theses, then we would have to assert examples and reasons that prove them, in which case we would become Autonomists. Therefore, there is no such thing as an "own system" for Consequentialists since [Nāgārjuna, Āryadeva, and Chandrakīrti] say that Mādhyamikas have no position and no thesis. As Nagarjuna's *Refutation of Objections* says:

> If I had any thesis,
> Then I would have that fault.
> Because I have no thesis,
> I am only faultless...

*Response:* If this which you propound is not the Middle Way system, then it is contradictory to establish it through citing passages from the Superior [Nāgārjuna] and his spiritual sons. Also, since [according to you] it cannot be posited as Chandrakīrti's or any other Buddhist system, it would be outside this [Buddhist] religion. [However] if you say that it is Middle Way and, from within that, the system of Chandrakīrti, then it would contradict [your assertion] that Proponents of the Middle [in general] and Chandrakīrti [in particular] do not have their own system.

Likewise, it is not feasible to propound—in hopes of being freed from assertions—that all presentations are solely from others' viewpoints. For in saying, "The existence of forms and so forth should be asserted solely from the viewpoint of others," though you do not assert the existence of forms and so forth, you certainly must assert a positing from others' viewpoint, in which case you are not freed from assertions. Since at that time you must assert the others from whose viewpoint [these presentations] are posited, as well as the positers, and so forth, to propound that assertions are made solely from the viewpoint of others not only does not help but harms your [position of] not having your own system.

And mistaken are the Consequentialists' assertions that wrong conceptions are overcome even though an ascertaining consciousness is not generated, and so forth.

[This system of tenets] is not wrong [in asserting] that all phenomena included within apprehended-object and apprehending-subject do not truly exist and that even the mere absence of true existence is not truly established,[a] and so forth.

These two, Proponents of Mind-Only and Middle Way Proponents of Self-Emptiness, do not assert in their own systems the mystery of the matrix-of-One-Gone-to-Bliss[b] and a self-cognizing and self-illuminating ultimate pristine wisdom.[c]

> Döl-b̄o-b̄a's *Mountain Doctrine* (106-107) explains away Chandrakīrti's objections to such a matrix-of-One-Gone-to-Bliss as confined to opinions earlier in his life and even cites contrary evidence in Chandrakīrti's *Supplement:*
>
> *Objection:* Is it not that the matrix-of-One-Gone-Thus is refuted by the master Chandrakīrti in the *Supplement to (Nāgārjuna's) "Treatise on the Middle"*?
>
> *Answer:* He clearly teaches it in his *Clear Lamp Commentary on the Guhyasamāja* because he says:
>
>> The syllable *oṃ* is the matrix-of-One-Gone-Thus. Since it gives rise to the unbreakable body of the yogi, it causes attainment of the vajra body.
>
> and:
>
>> The abode of all Buddhas is all sentient beings because of being the matrix-of-One-Gone-Thus.

---

[a] In the Great Middle Way also, self-emptiness—that is to say, the mere absence of true establishment—is not truly established. However, other-emptiness, the actual ultimate, is truly established.

[b] *bde gshegs snying po'i nges gsang.* Although Ge-luk-b̄as assert a matrix-of-One-Gone-to-Bliss that is the emptiness of inherent existence of a mind that is associated with defilement, they do not assert a matrix-of-One-Gone-to-Bliss endowed with ultimate Buddha-qualities of body, speech, and mind, whereas such is asserted in the Great Middle Way.

[c] *don dam ye shes rang rig rang gsal.*

and so forth. Even in the *Supplement to (Nāgārjuna's) "Treatise on the Middle"* Chandrakīrti says:

> Whether Buddhas arise or not,
> In actuality the emptiness
> Of all things is proclaimed
> As other-factuality.
>
> Limit of reality and thusness
> Are the emptiness of other-factuality.

[and Chandrakīrti's own commentary says,] "Other-factuality is the supreme suchness. Its supremacy is just its permanent existence."[a] Since such also appears, it is

---

[a] Chandrakīrti gives a triple explanation of other-factuality as supreme, other, and transcendent (see Louis de La Vallée Poussin, *Madhyamakāvatāra par Candrakīrti,* Bibliotheca Buddhica 9 [Osnabrück, Germany: Biblio Verlag, 1970], 339-340). Döl-b̄o-b̄a reads this as referring to three qualities of other-emptiness, whereas D̄zong-ka-b̄a (*Illumination of the Thought* [Sarnath, India: Pleasure of Elegant Sayings Press, 1973], 439.13) sees it as explaining that "other-factuality" itself has three meanings:

- The emptiness of inherent existence (*rang bzhin stong pa nyid*) is **supreme** in the sense that it exists without ever deviating from the character of suchness.
- The non-conceptual pristine wisdom, the excellent supramundane pristine wisdom, is **other**, and the emptiness of inherent existence is the object realized by that pristine wisdom.
- The emptiness of inherent existence is **transcendent** in that "transcendent" refers to the limit of reality which here is the nirvāṇa that is the extinction of cyclic existence.

Thus, for D̄zong-ka-b̄a, the passage is not about other-emptiness. He then is forced to explain the purpose of this separate emptiness since it repeats the emptiness of inherent existence, saying that it is for the sake of eliminating the qualm that suchness would truly exist if one asserted that it is the fundamental disposition of things, that it exists forever, and that it is the object of comprehension of

> suitable to analyze whether he speaks in self-contradiction. I wonder if earlier during his period of philosophical studies he generated qualms [about the matrix-of-One-Gone-Thus], but later through entering into profound secret mantra his mental development emerged, and his tenets changed.

Due to not having heard information[a] about these, earlier masters did not refute other-emptiness. However, later followers made refutations,[b] but not even a single one of them understood the essentials of the tenets of other-emptiness, and hence these are solely refutations in which the opposing position has not been apprehended.

### *Great Middle Way*

The Great Middle Way is the Middle Way School of Cognition,[c] renowned in Tibet as Other-Emptiness. It is illuminated by the texts of the foremost holy Maitreya,[d] by the Superior Asaṅga,[e] and by the supreme scholar Vasubandhu[f] and is greatly illuminated also

---

non-conceptual pristine wisdom. All three of these points as well as the implication that suchness truly or ultimately exists reflect Döl-b̄o-b̄a's and Tāranātha's opinion.

[a] *gnas tshul ma go ba.*

[b] In his *Autocommentary on the "Supplement"* Chandrakīrti explains that the teaching of a matrix-of-One-Gone-to-Bliss endowed with ultimate Buddha-qualities of body, speech, and mind requires interpretation, and D̄zong-ka-b̄a takes Döl-b̄o-b̄a's presentation of other-emptiness as his main opponent in his *The Essence of Eloquence;* see Hopkins, *Emptiness in the Mind-Only School of Buddhism,* 54ff., and *Reflections on Reality,* Part Four.

[c] *rnam rig gi dbu ma.*

[d] Döl-b̄o-b̄a cites all Five Doctrines of Maitreya in *Mountain Doctrine.*

[e] In *Mountain Doctrine* Döl-b̄o-b̄a cites Asaṅga's *Explanation of (Maitreya's) "Sublime Continuum of the Great Vehicle," Compendium of Bases, Grounds of Bodhisattvas, Summary of Manifest Knowledge,* and *Summary of the Great Vehicle.*

[f] In *Mountain Doctrine* Döl-b̄o-b̄a cites Vasubandhu's *Commentary on (Maitreya's) "Differentiation of the Middle and the Extremes," Explanation of*

in the Superior Nāgārjuna's *Praise of the Element of Attributes.*[a]

Döl-b̄o-b̄a's *Mountain Doctrine* (102-105):

*Objection:* Although others assert the matrix-of-One-Gone-to-Bliss as of definitive meaning, it is not so asserted in the Middle Way School.

*Answer:* The honorable Superior Nāgārjuna asserts it. His *Praise of the Element of Attributes* says:[b]

Homage and obeisance to [the sole jewel,] the element of attributes,
Definitely dwelling [pervasively] in all sentient beings,
Which if one does not thoroughly know [with pristine wisdom],
One wanders in the three existences.

From having purified [by means of the path the defilements of] just that [element of attributes]
Which serves as the cause of cyclic existence [due to being associated with adventitious defilement],
That very [element of attributes] purified [of defilement] is nirvāṇa.
The body of attributes also is just that.

[Due to being mixed with limitless defilement, the element of attributes is not seen;
For example,] just as due to being mixed with milk,
The essence of butter is not seen,
So due to being mixed with afflictive emotions
The element of attributes also is not seen.

[From purifying defilement, it is seen;
For example,] just as due to having purified milk

---

*(Maitreya's) "Ornament for the Great Vehicle Sūtras," Principles of Explanation, The Thirty,* and commentaries on the Perfection of Wisdom Sūtras attributed to Vasubandhu in Jo-nang and to Daṃṣhṭasena in Ge-luk.

[a] *chos kyi dbyings su bstod pa, dharmadhātustotra;* P2010, vol. 46.

[b] P2010, vol. 46, 31.3.7-31.4.6; brackets are from Döl-b̄o-b̄a Shay-rap-gyel-tsen's *[Interlinear Commentary on Nāgārjuna's] "Praise of the Element of Attributes,"* 1b.2ff.

The essence of butter [is seen] without [obstructive] defilement,
So due to having purified [and extinguished] the afflictive emotions [through the path]
The very undefiled element of attributes [is manifestly seen].

[During the basal state of a sentient being, for example,]
Just as a butter-lamp dwelling inside a pot
Is not in the least perceived,
So the element of attributes also
Is not perceived inside the pot of afflictive emotions.

[During the path] from whatsoever directions [of proceeding on the grounds and paths]
Holes in the pot [of afflictive emotions] protrude,
From just those directions
A nature of [clear] light arises.

[Finally] when by the vajra meditative stabilization
The [obstructive] pot has [entirely] been broken,
[The element of attributes] illuminates
[And is seen] to the ends of space.

[Would the element of attributes which has ceased while one is a sentient being and is produced at the time of the path and fruit not be compounded?]
The element of attributes is not [newly] produced,
[And its entity] never ceases [while one is a sentient being].
At all times [during the basal state, the path, and the fruit] it is without afflictive emotions [in its nature]—
In the beginning [in the basal state], the middle [during the path], and the end [during the fruit primordially] free from defilement [in its nature].

[If the element of attributes exists luminously without ever being produced or ceasing, then why is it that all sentient beings, Bodhisattvas, and Buddhas without distinction do not see it as luminous?]
Just as a *vaiḍūrya* gem
At all times is luminous
But dwelling inside an [obstructive] stone
Its light is not manifest [to anyone],

So the element of attributes obscured
By afflictive emotions is very undefiled [in its nature],
But its light is not manifest in the cyclic existence [of afflictive emotions],
Becoming [manifestly] luminous in nirvāṇa.

and:

[Although the element of attributes is naturally pure, it is obstructed by obstructing factors;
For example,] even the undefiled sun and moon
Are obscured by five obstructions—
Clouds, mist, smoke,
The face of rāhu, and dust and the like.

Similarly, the mind of clear light [which is the nature of all sentient beings]
Is obscured by five obstructions—
Desire, harmful intent, laziness,
Excitement, and doubt.

[Therefore, although a Buddha in which all qualities such as the powers and so forth are integrally complete exists primordially in all sentient beings, the defilements are extinguished through striving at the path clearing away obstructions, but the clear light is not consumed; for example,]
When a garment [made from a hard mineral] that is stained
With various defilements and to be cleansed [of defilement] by fire

Is put in fire, its stains
Are burned but it is not.

So, similarly, with regard to the mind of clear light
Which has the stains of desire and so forth,
Its stains are burned by the fire of wisdom [on the path]
But [since it does not burn the clear light, the qualities of the clear light do not become non-existent the way iron is consumed or worn away, and hence] that [path] does not [burn away] the clear light.

[Well then, since the sūtras teaching emptiness spoken by the Conqueror indicate that all are emptiness, do they not refute that even the clear light is in the mode of being?]
All the sūtras [such as the Mother Sūtras and so forth]
Spoken by the Conqueror that teach emptiness
Overcome the afflictive emotions [of conceiving self]
But do not diminish [and refute] the essential constituent.

[Ultimately the element of attributes cannot be refuted;
For example,] just as water existing on the sphere of earth
Resides [in its nature] without defilement,
So the pristine wisdom inside afflictive emotions
Similarly [always] abides without defilement [never suitable to be non-existent].

and:

[Though it exists, it is not seen if the obstructions are not purified;
For example,] just as a child exists in the belly
Of the womb but is not seen,
So the element of attributes covered
With afflictive emotions also is not seen [though always resident].

and:

> [A single river has different states due to relation with other causes and conditions;]
> Just as a river in summer
> Is said to be "warm"
> But that [same river] itself in cold season
> Is said to be "cold,"
>
> So when [the element of attributes is] covered with the nets of afflictive emotions,
> It is called "sentient being,"
> But when that [element of attributes] itself is separated from afflictive emotions,
> It is called "Buddha."

and so forth. Hence, by way of many examples Nāgārjuna speaks at length of the matrix-of-One-Gone-to-Bliss that is equivalent to the element of attributes, body of attributes, mind of natural clear light, self-arisen pristine wisdom, and so forth.

Therefore, the assertion of both of the supreme Superiors [that is, Asaṅga and Nāgārjuna] is other-emptiness.

In this system, the truthless[a] [that is, those lacking true existence] are in brief:

1. all *basal* phenomena of cyclic existence—non-things[b] (that is, imputed uncompounded phenomena,[c] such as the three uncompounded phenomena[d] asserted in the Mind-Only School

---

[a] *bden med.*

[b] *dngos med, abhāva.*

[c] *'dus ma byas btags pa ba.* These are called "imputed" because the actual uncompounded is the ultimate truth according to the Great Middle Way, as Tāranātha explicitly says in the *Twenty-one Differences Regarding the Profound Meaning,* 127.

[d] The three renowned uncompounded phenomena are uncompounded space, analytical cessations, and non-analytical cessations. The latter two are to be distinguished from ultimate true cessations.

and below), forms and so forth[a] that are renowned to be external objects,[b] the eight collections of consciousness,[c] the fifty-one mental factors,[d] and so forth

2. all temporary phenomena included within *paths*
3. from among those included within the *fruit,* Buddhahood,

---

[a] These are forms, feelings, discriminations, compositional factors, and consciousnesses. Included within the first are visible forms, sounds, odors, tastes, tangible objects, eye sense-power, ear sense-power, nose sense-power, tongue sense-power, and body sense-power.

[b] *phyi don, bāhyārtha.* The specification of "external objects" is likely for the sake of excluding empty forms (*stong gzugs*), which are ultimates and truly established. As Döl-b̄o-b̄a (*Mountain Doctrine,* 215) says:

> Also, the *Mahāparinirvāṇa Sūtra* makes pronouncements within differentiating well between empty forms, and so forth, and non-empty forms, and so forth:
>
> > Kauṇḍinya, empty form—due to the condition of ceasing—attains release in the aspect of non-empty form. This should be known in extension likewise with regard to feelings, discriminations, compositional factors, and consciousnesses.
>
> Concerning those, respectively the forms and so forth of adventitious defilements are empty of their own entities—an emptiness of non-entities—and the forms and so forth of the matrix-of-One-Gone-to-Bliss are the ultimate, other-emptiness, emptiness that is the [ultimate] nature of non-entities.

[c] The eight consciousnesses are the eye consciousness, ear consciousness, nose consciousness, tongue consciousness, body consciousness, mental consciousness, afflicted mentality, and mind-basis-of-all. Döl-b̄o-b̄a (*Mountain Doctrine,* 235) holds that these are also taught in Great Middle Way:

> Those who assert that Maitreya's *Differentiation of the Middle and the Extremes* and so forth are proprietary texts of Mind-Only by reason of the fact that they teach the three natures, eight collections of consciousness, and so forth are mistaken, because these are also taught in sūtras and tantras of the final Middle Way.

[d] See p. 34, and Hopkins, *Meditation on Emptiness,* 238-268.

> newly arisen factors[a] and those [phenomena] included within the other-appearance[b] of trainees

that is to say, all appearing and renowned phenomena, or phenomena in the division of phenomena and noumenon,[c] or all phenomena included within apprehended-object and apprehending-subject, or—on this occasion of delineating the ultimate—all effective things and non-things, namely, all that are compounded and adventitiously posited.[d]

Self-cognizing, self-illuminating pristine wisdom[e] that is non-dual with the basic element is called the ultimate truth, the uncompounded noumenon.

> Döl-b̄o-b̄a's *Mountain Doctrine* (403-404):
>
> *Objection:* The noumenon is the object to be known, and pristine wisdom is the subject knowing it; hence it is not feasible for those two to be equivalent, as is the case with a form and an eye consciousness.
>
> *Answer:* There is no fault:
>
> - because the non-sameness of knower and object known is for conventional other-cognition, whereas ultimate self-cognizing knower and object known are the same
> - and because the element of attributes itself is pristine

---

[a] *gsar du byung ba'i cha.* These are produced fruits (*bskyed pa'i 'bras bu*), that is to say, effects produced by the spiritual path as opposed to separative fruits (*bral ba'i 'bras bu*), which are merely uncovered by the path and thus already existent factors that need only to be separated from defilement.

[b] *gzhan snang.* These are displays by Buddhas in accordance with the dispositions and needs of trainees and thus are compounded, impermanent, and conventional. See especially the quotes from Maitreya's *Sublime Continuum of the Great Vehicle* in the fruit section of Döl-b̄o-b̄a's *Mountain Doctrine,* 492-511.

[c] *chos dang chos nyid.*

[d] *glo bur bar gzhag pa.* Even non-things are compounded, since only the ultimate is actually uncompounded; see p. 127.

[e] *ye shes rang rig rang gsal.*

wisdom cognizing itself by itself (*rang gis rang rig pa'i ye shes*), the ultimate mind of enlightenment, undifferentiable emptiness and compassion, undifferentiable method and wisdom, and undifferentiable bliss and emptiness

- and because the union of those into one is the androgynous state (*ma ning gi go 'phang*)...

Döl-b̄o-b̄a's *Mountain Doctrine* (300): That which is self-arisen pristine wisdom, ultimate truth, abiding pervasively in all does not differ in anyone as to its natural purity, but through the force of persons there are the differences of purity from adventitious defilements and of impurity due to adventitious defilements, like the fact that the sole sky—which by its own nature does not exist as entities of clouds and is purified of entities of clouds—is not purified of clouds in some areas and is purified of clouds in other areas. Therefore, it is not contradictory that just as sky that is not purified of clouds does not exist in any area, so sky that is purified of clouds does not exist in any area, but, due to the area, there is impure sky and there is pure sky. Similarly, while the naturally pure, sole, basic element of the ultimate abides together with defilements in some persons and abides without defilements in some, it is posited as the basis and the fruit through the force of the presence or the absence of defilements in persons, [but] the entity of the noumenon does not differ.

Hence, persons who have abandoned all adventitious defilements have no need to again practice true paths because they have completed training, and they have already attained the body of ultimate pristine wisdom. Persons other than them just need to practice true paths properly because although the final Buddha integrally abides in them, it has not been attained because of being obstructed by adventitious defilements.

Moreover, this cultivation of the path is not for the sake of **producing** a body of attributes:

- because the uncompounded basic element that has an immutable nature is not fit to be produced by any causes and conditions
- and because it has abided always primordially with a spontaneous nature without needing to be produced
- and because if though existent, it needed to be produced, it most absurdly would need to be produced endlessly.

It is only truly established, able to bear analysis by reasoning.[a] They assert that because, when analyzed, the space-like [absence of true establishment] asserted by the Proponents of Self-Emptiness is a non-thing,[b] it is not the ultimate truth.[c] These tenets are flawless

---

[a] In his *Twenty-one Differences Regarding the Profound Meaning* (133) Tāranātha specifies this as "the reasoning of dependent-arising, the lack of being one or many, and so forth."

Döl-b̄o-b̄a (213) defines self-emptiness as meaning that phenomena "that cannot withstand analysis and finally disintegrate are empty of their own entities." Thus, for him also, pristine wisdom is able to bear analysis; Tāranātha calls this capacity to bear analysis "true establishment," whereas in *Mountain Doctrine* Döl-b̄o-b̄a favors "ultimate establishment." Since the ultimate exists or is found by such analysis, it is said to ultimately exist or truly exist.

To counter this notion Ge-luk-b̄a scholars make the distinction that although emptiness is the ultimate truth because it is found by ultimate analysis, it does not ultimately or truly exist in that when it is taken as the object of analysis, it itself cannot bear analysis by reasoning; see the extensive explanation (Hopkins, *Maps of the Profound,* 737ff.) at the point of commenting on Jam-ȳang-shay-b̄a's root text:

> Whatever truly exists must exist in the perspective of reasoning because of being truly established. But what exists for that is not necessarily truly established, like the noumenon. Although there are objects found by a rational consciousness, what is able to bear analysis by it must stand to be truly established because true establishment is being analyzed. Establishment as bearing analysis by a rational consciousness is true establishment, the object of negation here.

[b] *dngos med.*

[c] See Döl-b̄o-b̄a's long exposition that self-emptiness is not the

and endowed with all good qualities.

All those proponents of the Great Vehicle [that is, the Mind-Only School, the Ordinary Middle Way School, and the Great Middle Way] assert all Great Vehicle sūtras as the word of Buddha, but:

- The Proponents of Mind-Only hold the *Sūtra Unraveling the Thought,*[a] the *Descent into Laṅkā Sūtra,*[b] the *Sūtra on the Heavily Adorned Array,*[c] and the *Buddhāvataṃsaka Sūtra*[d] to be of definitive meaning[e] and assert that the others require interpretation.[f] The authors of this tenet system[g] are five hundred earlier masters.
- Those holding the Ordinary Middle Way School propound that all sūtras of the final wheel of doctrine require interpretation and that the Perfection of Wisdom Sūtras of the middle wheel of doctrine are the finality of the definitive. Those ascertained as the authors of this tenet system[h] are just those mentioned above, Buddhapālita and so forth. According to their own assertions,[i] they assert that the eight Proponents of Non-Nature, such as Rāhulabhadra [that is, Saraha] and even the master Nāgārjuna, hold only this tenet system.[j]

---

ultimate in *Mountain Doctrine* in a section titled "Extensive explanation of damage to the assertion that self-emptiness, the ultimate, and so forth are synonyms," 254-315.

a *dgongs pa nges par 'grel pa'i mdo, saṃdhinirmocanasūtra;* P774, vol. 29.

b *lang kar gshegs pa'i mdo, laṅkāvatārasūtra;* P775, vol. 29.

c *rgyan stug po bkod pa'i mdo, ghanavyūhasūtra;* P778, vol. 29.

d *sangs rgyas phal po che zhes bya ba shin tu rgyas pa chen po'i mdo, buddhāvataṃsakanāma-mahāvaipulyasūtra;* P761, vols. 25-26.

e *nges don, nītārtha.*

f *drang don, neyārtha.*

g *grub mtha' byed pa po.*

h *grub mtha' byed pa po yin nges.*

i *'di rnams kyi rang rig gi 'dod pas;* translation doubtful.

j Tāranātha's point is that, despite this claim, Nāgārjuna and so forth are actually Proponents of Other-Emptiness. As he says later (92), "That Bhāvaviveka, Buddhapālita, and so forth are renowned as Proponents of Self-Emptiness and Proponents of Non-Nature is a case of mainly taking

- Those of the Great Middle Way rely on all sūtras of the three stages of wheels of doctrine. In particular, in reliance on (1) many sūtras of the first wheel of doctrine such as the *Sūtra of Advice to Katyāyana*[a] and the *Great Sūtra on Emptiness,*[b] (2) many sūtras of the middle period wheel of doctrine, such as the Questions of Maitreya Chapter[c] and the *Five Hundred Stanza Perfection of Wisdom Sūtra,*[d] and (3) many sūtras of the final wheel of doctrine, such as the four sūtras[e] and so forth, they composed common, coarse tenets teaching that the noumenon is truly established.

Döl-b̄o-b̄a's *Mountain Doctrine* (231):

*Objection:* Since the final wheel of doctrine together with the *Sūtra Unraveling the Thought* are proprietary texts of the Proponents of Mind-Only, the explanation that they are the final Middle Way is not right.

*Answer:* There are no pure sources indicating that those are proprietary texts of the Proponents of Mind-Only.

*Objection:* They are proprietary texts of Mind-Only because the three natures are taught in them.

*Answer:* In that case, the *Mother of the Conquerors* [that is, the Perfection of Wisdom Sūtras] would be proprietary

---

what is renowned to the ordinary world."

[a] In Pāli this is the *Kaccayanagotta Sutta.*

[b] In Pāli this is the *Mahasuññata Sutta.*

[c] Cyrus R. Stearns (*The Buddha from Dolpo: A Study of the Life and Thought of the Tibetan Master Dolpopa Sherab Gyaltsen* [Albany, N.Y.: State University of New York Press, 1999], 218 n. 29) identifies this as the seventy-second chapter of the *Twenty-Five Thousand Stanza Perfection of Wisdom Sūtra* and the eighty-third chapter of *Eighteen Thousand Stanza Perfection of Wisdom Sūtra* and states that a Questions of Maitreya Chapter "is not found in other versions of the *Prajñāpāramitā.*"

[d] *'phags pa shes rab kyi pha rol tu phyin pa lnga brgya pa, āryapañca-śatikāprajñāpāramitā;* P0738, vol. 21.

[e] These are the *Sūtra Unraveling the Thought,* the *Descent into Laṅkā Sūtra,* the *Heavily Adorned Array,* and the *Buddhāvataṃsaka Sūtra,* which were mentioned above in connection with the Mind-Only School.

texts of Mind-Only, because the three natures are taught in them. Moreover, the *Medium Length Mother* [that is, the *Twenty-five Thousand Stanza Perfection of Wisdom Sūtra*] says:

> The Supramundane Victor said to the Bodhisattva Maitreya, "Maitreya, Bodhisattvas practicing the perfection of wisdom and dwelling in skill with regard to distinguishing phenomena should know to designate distinctions of forms by way of three aspects, and they should know to designate distinctions with regard to feelings, discriminations, compositional factors, and consciousnesses through to the qualities of Buddhahood as follows: This is imputational form; this is imputed form; this is noumenal form.

It similarly applies this at length to feelings, discriminations, compositional factors, and consciousnesses through to the qualities of Buddhahood. Respectively, these are imputational, other-powered, and thoroughly established forms.

Moreover, that same text says that the basis of the emptiness of the imputational nature and of the other-powered nature is the basic element of the ultimate, the thoroughly established nature:

> Whether the Ones-Gone-Thus appear or not, the noumenon and the basic element of the source of attributes just abide. The noumenon's forms are imputed forms' absence of the nature of imputational forms and absence of a self of phenomena—suchness and limit of reality—for permanent, permanent time and stable, stable time. These are the noumenon's feelings, discriminations, compositional factors, and consciousnesses through to the noumenon's qualities of a Buddha." Thus Buddha said.

and moreover the same text speaks of how the three natures are set forth within applying such through to the qualities of Buddhahood:

> Maitreya, these imputational forms [that is to say, the ultimate existence imagined in forms] should be viewed as not substantially existing [because of not existing at all]. These imputed forms [that is, forms themselves] should be viewed as substantially existing because conceptuality substantially exists and not because forms operate under their own power. Noumenal forms should be viewed as neither not substantially existing nor as substantially existing but as distinguished by being the ultimate.

and so forth.

- And, similarly, in reliance on many sūtras teaching the finality of definitive meanings, such as the *Matrix-of-One-Gone-Thus Sūtra,*[a] the *Great Drum Sūtra,*[b] the *Aṅgulimāla Sūtra,*[c] the *Shrīmālādevī Sūtra,*[d] the *Mahāparinirvāṇa Sūtra,*[e] the *Cloud of Jewels Sūtra,*[f] the *Magical Meditative Stabilization Ascertaining Peace Sūtra,*[g] and so forth, those of the Great Middle Way composed—as secret discourse—the detailed, uncommon tenets that just that basic element of reality, the matrix of One-Gone-Thus, the body of attributes, the permanent-stable-

---

[a] *'phags pa de bzhin gshegs pa'i snying po zhes bya ba theg pa chen po'i mdo, āryatathāgatagarbhanāmamahāyanasūtra;* P924, vol. 36.

[b] *rnga bo che chen po'i mdo, mahābherī haraka parivarta;* P888, vol. 35.

[c] *sor mo'i phreng ba la phan pa'i mdo, aṅgulimālīyasūtra;* P879, vol. 34.

[d] *lha mo dpal 'phreng gi seng ge'i sgra'i mdo, śrīmālādevīsiṃhanādasūtra;* P760.48, vol. 24. See the translation in Alex Wayman and Hideko Wayman, *The Lion's Roar of Queen Śrīmālā: A Buddhist Scripture on the Tathāgatagarbha Theory* (New York: Columbia University Press, 1974).

[e] *yongs su mya ngan las 'das pa chen po'i mdo, mahāparinirvāṇasūtra;* P788, vol. 31; see Kosho Yamamoto, *The Mahāyāna Mahāparinirvāṇa-sutra* (Ube, Japan: Karinbunko, 1973).

[f] *dkon mchog sprin gyi mdo, ratnameghasūtra;* P879, vol. 35.

[g] *rab tu zhi ba rnam par nges pa'i cho 'phrul gyi ting nge 'dzin gyi mdo, praśāntaviniścayaprātihāryanāmasamādhisūtra;* P797, vol. 32. Döl-b̄o-b̄a cites all seven of these sūtras; see the index in *Mountain Doctrine.*

eternal,[a] and all ultimate[b] Buddha-qualities primordially in-dwell intrinsically.

Döl-b̄o-b̄a's *Mountain Doctrine* (185-188):

*Objection:* If the ultimate Buddha intrinsically exists in all sentient beings, then they intrinsically would have final abandonment [of defilements] and have final realization [of the truth].

*Answer:* This must be taught upon making a distinction. Hence, there are two types of abandonment—abandonment of all defilements that is their primordial absence of inherent establishment and extinguishment of adventitious defilements upon their being overcome by antidotes...Although the second abandonment [that is, the extinguishment of adventitious defilements upon being overcome by antidotes] does not exist in sentient beings who have not cultivated the path, this does not involve a fault in our tenets, because it is not asserted that all sentient beings are Buddhas or have attained Buddhahood and because it is not asserted that conventional Buddhahood exists in all sentient beings.

Similarly, there are also two types of Buddha-realization, the self-arisen pristine wisdom that is the primordial realization of the noumenon—knowing itself by itself—and the other-arisen pristine wisdom that is realization produced from having cultivated the profound path...

Therefore, since the first type of realization [that is, self-arisen pristine wisdom that is primordial realization of the noumenon] is indivisibly complete in the noumenon, it is the case that where that noumenon exists, this realization also exists. Although the second type of realization [which is produced from having cultivated the profound path] is not complete in sentient beings who have not

a *rtag brtan g.yung drung.*

b Tāranātha specifies *ultimate* Buddha-qualities because conventional Buddha-qualities are produced through practice of the path and hence do not primordially reside in the continuums of sentient beings.

> entered the path and although they have not directly realized selflessness, this does not involve a fault in our tenets; the reasons are as before...
>
> Therefore, very many distorted challenges such as, "If Buddha exists in sentient beings, all karmas, afflictive emotions, and sufferings would not exist," and so forth, and "Sentient beings would realize all knowables," and so forth are babble by those who do not know the difference between existence [that is, presence] and being such and such. This is because existence does not establish being such and such. If it did, then since explanations exist in humans, are humans explanations?

The author of texts illuminating the meaning of the sūtras is the regent, the Superior Maitreya. In his *Ornament for Clear Realization* he sets this forth briefly with rough religious vocabulary; in his *Ornament for the Great Vehicle Sūtras, Differentiation of the Middle and the Extremes,* and *Differentiation of Phenomena and Noumenon* he speaks about it clearly and extensively; and in his *Sublime Continuum of the Great Vehicle* he delineates the detailed, uncommon tenets that are the meaning of the sūtras on the matrix.

The authors of commentaries on the thought of those texts are Asaṅga and Vasubandhu. In Asaṅga's *Explanation of (Maitreya's) "Sublime Continuum of the Great Vehicle,"* the uncommon tenets are very vast and clear, and, in general, the Middle Way of Other-Emptiness is clear in all of the treatises by the two brothers [Asaṅga and Vasubandhu]. In Vasubandhu's *Commentary on the Twenty-Five Thousand Stanza Perfection of Wisdom Sūtra: Conquest Over Objections,*[a] and *Commentary on (Maitreya's) "Differentiation of*

---

[a] This is the *Commentary on the One Hundred Thousand, Twenty-Five Thousand, and Eighteen Thousand Stanza Perfection of Wisdom Sūtras* called *Conquest over Harm to the Three Mother Scriptures* (*'phags pa shes rab kyi pha rol tu phyin pa 'bum pa dang nyi khri lnga stong pa dang khri brgyad stong pa'i rgya cher bshad pa, āryaśatasāhasrikāpañcaviṃsatisāhasrikā-aṣṭadaśasāhasrikāprajñāpāramitābṛhaṭṭīkā / yum gsum gnod 'joms;* P5206, vol. 93. D̄zong-ka-b̄a challenges the assertion that this text is by Vasubandhu, holding that it is actually by Daṃṣhṭasena (*mche ba'i sde*), also known as *Daṃṣṭrāsena, Diṣṭasena, Daṃṣṭasena, Daṃṣṭrāsena,*

*Phenomena and Noumenon*" it is clear and extensive.[a]

The general tenets of other-emptiness are explained at length by many good students in the lineage of Dignāga, Sthiramati, and so forth, and the uncommon tenets, being difficult to fit in others' minds, were spread in the manner of transmission from ear to ear. Later, in dependence upon its happening that many in India confused this Middle Way of Other-Emptiness and the tenets of Mind-Only, most Tibetans mistook them to be the same. In Tibet, many translators and scholars translated texts, but those who purely held the tenets are those following the meditative system of the Doctrines of Maitreya[b]—the translators Su Ga-way-dor-jay,[c] D̄zen Kha-wo-che,[d] and so forth. In particular, the one who pervasively spread the profound other-emptiness on the earth with the roar of a lion is the great omniscient Döl-bu-b̄a[e] S̄hay-rap-gyel-tsen.

## II. Identifying the Presentation of the Middle

Maitreya's *Differentiation of the Middle and the Extremes* says:

> Unreal ideation exists.
> Duality does not exist there.
> Emptiness exists here.

---

*Daṃṣṭasyana,* and so forth; see Hopkins, *Emptiness in the Mind-Only School of Buddhism,* 225-233 (especially 231-233) and 335-341.

[a] For Döl-b̄o-b̄a's citations of these treatises, see the index to *Mountain Doctrine.*

[b] For the Five Doctrines of Maitreya see the Bibliography.

[c] *gzu dga' ba'i rdo rje.* Perhaps he is *gzu chos kyi rdo rje* mentioned in the next note.

[d] *btsan kha bo che,* born 1021. Gene Smith (TBRC) reports:

> 1076. Together with Rngog Blo-ldan-shes-rab, Rwa Lo Rdo-rje-grags-pa, Khyung-po Chos-kyi-brtson-'grus traveled to Kashmir to study with Sadzdza-na and others. Worked with Gzu Chos-kyi-rdo-rje.
>
> 1089. Return to Tibet and begins to teach the Byams chos sde lnga at Yar-stod Brag-rgya. His school of exegesis of the Byams chos sde lnga became known as the Btsan lugs.

[e] *dol bu pa;* also *dol po pa.*

Also that exists in that.

Not empty and not non-empty,
Thereby all are explained.
Due to existence and due to non-existence, existence.
Therefore that is the middle path.[a]

---

[a] I.1-1.2; P5522, vol. 108, 19.4.5. The Sanskrit, from Gadjin M. Nagao, *Madhyāntavibhāga-bhāṣya* (Tokyo: Suzuki Research Foundation, 1964), 17, is:

*abhūta-parikalpo 'sti dvayan tatra na vidyate/*
*śūnyatā vidyate tv atra tasyām api sa vidyate//*

*na śūnyaṃ nāpi cāśūnyaṃ tasmāt sarvvam [Pandeya: sarvaṃ] vidhīyate/*
*satvād asatvāt satvāc* [Pandeya: *sattvādasattvāt sattvāc*] *ca madhyamā pratipac ca sā//*

See also Ramchandra Pandeya, *Madhyānta-vibhāga-śāstra* (Delhi: Motilal Banarsidass, 1971), 9, 13. With bracketed additions reflecting Tāranātha's commentary, the stanzas read:

Unreal ideation exists [conventionally].
Duality [of apprehended-object and apprehending-subject and so forth] does not exist there [in ideation].
[The pristine wisdom of] emptiness [truly] exists here [in unreal ideation in the manner of being its noumenon].
Also that [unreal ideation] exists [as an entity without true existence] in that [noumenon].

[The noumenal wisdom is] not empty and [conventionalities are] not non-empty,
Thereby all are explained.
Due to the [the noumenal wisdom's true] existence and due to the non-existence [of change within it, it always] exists.
Therefore that is the middle path.

Dzong-ka-ba cites these stanzas in his *The Essence of Eloquence* (Hopkins, *Emptiness in the Mind-Only School of Buddhism,* 182); with bracketed additions reflecting his commentary, the stanzas read:

Unreal ideation [ideation being the main other-powered nature] exists [by way of its own character in that it is produced from causes and conditions].
Duality [of subject and object in accordance with their appearance

This is saying that:

> In terms of delineating obscurational truths,[a] mere unreal ideation[b]—that is to say, a consciousness to which various

as if distant and cut off] does not exist in that [ideation].

[The thoroughly established nature which is the] emptiness [of being distant and cut off] exists [by way of its own character as the mode of subsistence] in this [ideation].

Also that [ideation] exists [as an obstructor] to [realization of] that [emptiness].

[Thus, other-powered natures and thoroughly established natures] are not empty [of establishment by way of the object's own character] and are not non-empty [of subject and object being distant and cut off].

Thereby all [of the mode of thought in the teachings in the Perfection of Wisdom Sūtras, and so forth, of not being empty and of not being non-empty] is explained [thoroughly].

Due to the existence [of the other-powered nature that is the erroneous ideation apprehending object and subject as distant and cut off, the extreme of non-existence is avoided] and due to the non-existence [of distant and cut off object and subject—in accordance with how they are apprehended by that ideation—as their mode of subsistence, the extreme of existence is avoided, and ideation and emptiness] exist.

Therefore that [thoroughly established nature which is the emptiness of distant and cut off object and subject and which is the voidness of the two extremes in other-powered natures] is the middle path [that is to say, is established as the meaning of the middle].

[a] *kun rdzob bden pa, saṃvṛtisatya.*

[b] To unpack the term "unreal ideation" (*yang dag pa ma yin pa'i kun tu rtog pa / yang dag ma yin kun rtog, abhūtaparikalpa*) Döl-b̄o-b̄a (*Mountain Doctrine,* 530) cites Maitreya's *Differentiation of Phenomena and Noumenon:*

> Concerning this, the character of phenomena
> Is unreal ideation in which there is
> Appearance of duality and concordance with verbalization;
> Because the non-existent appears, it is *unreal.*
> Since all those are non-factual

appearances dawn—exists conventionally. However, the factor of the object apprehended and the factor of apprehender that appear to that [ideation] do not exist even conventionally, since they are merely mentally imputed.[a] Consequently, obscurational truths are released from the two extremes: ideation is released from the extreme of non-existence and from the extreme of annihilation through asserting that it conventionally exists, and ideation is released from the extreme of permanence and the extreme of existence through being beyond all superimposed factors of relative phenomena,[b] such as the factors of object apprehended and apprehender, and so forth.

The pristine wisdom of emptiness, beyond proliferation, truly exists in that unreal ideational consciousness in the manner of being its noumenon. On the occasion of defilement, those consciousnesses exist in that noumenon as subjects[c] [having as their nature the noumenon], entities without true existence—adventitious defilements suitable to separated, defilements to be abandoned. Consequently, ultimate truths also are "devoid of the two extremes": emptiness is truly established, and all phenomena included within the two, apprehended-object and apprehending-subject, such as ideation and so forth, are without true existence, and therefore [ultimate truths] are beyond the two extremes of existence and non-existence, permanence and annihilation.

Hence, conventionalities—the two, apprehended-object and apprehending-subject—except for only being the dawning of mistaken appearances, are empty of their own entities due to being unestablishable by way of their own entities.[d] And something established as an other-entity from within the division of the pair, self and other, does

---

And mere conceptualization, it is *ideation.*

a *blos btags pa tsam.*

b *ltos chos.*

c *chos can.*

d *rang gi ngo bos grub rgyu med pa.*

not occur among objects of knowledge. Therefore, conventionalities are empty in all respects and hence are not non-empty.[a] The noumenal wisdom is primordially established by way of its own nature and never changes; hence, it is not empty of its own entity and always exists.

> Döl-b̄o-b̄a's *Mountain Doctrine* (329): Concerning this, whereas conventional phenomena do not at all exist in the mode of subsistence, the extreme of existence is the superimposition that they do. Whereas the partless, omnipresent pristine wisdom of the element of attributes always abides pervading all, the extreme of non-existence is the deprecation that it does not exist and is not established and is empty of its own entity. That which is the middle devoid of those extremes is the basis devoid of all extremes such as existence and non-existence, superimposition, and deprecation, permanence and annihilation, and so forth, due to which it is the Final Great Middle. It is non-material emptiness, emptiness far from an annihilatory emptiness, great emptiness that is the ultimate pristine wisdom of Superiors, five immutable great emptinesses, six immutable empty drops, *a* which is the supreme of all letters, Buddha earlier than all Buddhas, primordially released One-Gone-Thus, causeless original Buddha, aspectlessness endowed with all aspects—insuperable and not fit to be abandoned. Not to be deprecated, it is the inconceivable element of attributes beyond phenomena of consciousness and not in the sphere of argument; it is to be realized in individual self-cognition by yogis.
>
> Consequently, those who come to the conclusion that:
>
> - the "middle" is exhausted as designated to the mere voidness of all extremes
> - "even the middle is empty of the middle"
> - "even the ultimate is empty of the ultimate"

---

[a] No object is other than itself and thus nothing is established as an other-entity. Hence, since conventionalities both lack establishment as other entities and lack self-establishment, they are empty in all respects.

> and so forth do not accord with the thought of the Conqueror because, for the character of the emptiness that is the final mode of subsistence, the mere emptiness of non-entities is not sufficient. Rather, the emptiness that is the [ultimate] nature of non-entities [that is, emptiness that is the ultimate nature opposite from non-entities] is required.

*Objection:* But do the sūtras not say that even the element of attributes is empty?

*Answer:* In general, despite being empty or being an emptiness, it is not necessary that it is empty of its own entity.[a] Pristine wisdom is said to be "emptiness"[b] because it is empty of all proliferations that have the character of anything other than itself or is empty of all apprehended-objects and apprehending-subjects.

> Döl-b̄o-b̄a's *Mountain Doctrine* (364-368):[c] For the *Sūtra Unraveling the Thought* says:
>
> > Based on just the naturelessness of all phenomena and based on just the absence of production, the absence of cessation, quiescence from the start, and naturally passed beyond sorrow, the Supramundane Victor turned a second wheel of doctrine, for those engaged in the Great Vehicle, very fantastic and marvelous, through the aspect of speaking on emptiness. Furthermore, that wheel of doctrine turned by the Supramundane Victor is surpassable, affords an occasion [for refutation], requires interpretation, and serves as a basis for controversy.

---

a *rang gi ngo bos stong pa.*

b *stong pa nyid.*

c Döl-b̄o-b̄a's answer to this same objection is twofold: first he explains that such statements of self-emptiness require interpretation and then he explains, as Tāranātha does, that all such statements do not necessarily speak of self-emptiness, for some indicate other-emptiness. It seems to me that Tāranātha takes for granted the first explanation when he says "although [something] is empty or is an emptiness, it is not *necessary* that it be empty of its own entity."

Similarly, it should be understood that all statements—in these and those texts of the middle wheel of doctrine—of the non-self-empty as self-empty are just of interpretable meaning with a thought behind them. [Understanding] this depends on the lamp of unique quintessential instructions of good differentiation [found in the three cycles of Bodhisattva commentaries].

Here the **purpose** of speaking in consideration of such is to thoroughly pacify apprehension, discrimination, and conceptualization of the element of attributes and so forth as this or that. About the **damage** to their being of definitive meaning, it is because:

- the element of attributes, thusness, limit of reality, and so forth are all said to be ultimate deities, mantras, tantras, maṇḍalas, and mudrās—the final Buddha, four bodies, five wisdoms, letter *e, bhaga,* source of attributes, water-born [that is, lotus], secrecy, great secrecy, letter *a,* perfection-of-wisdom-goddess, vishvamātā, vajravarahī, and so forth; the syllable *vaṃ,* great bliss, drop, vajra, heruka, suchness, self-arisen Buddha, and so forth; Vajradhara, Vajrasattva, the syllables *evaṃ,* Kālachakra, Vajrabhairava, Vajraishvara, Chakrasaṃvara, Guhyasamāja, Hevajra, and so forth—and those also are said to be the noumenon, thusness, and so forth
- and those are said to be entities of endless attributes such as the powers, fearlessnesses, and so forth that are non-self-empty qualities.

Here, with regard to the **basis in [Buddha's] thought**, such was said in consideration that all [conceptual] apprehensions as those (that is, as the element of attributes and so forth) and all subjects involved with those [conceptual apprehensions] are self-empty. This is because all phenomena, forms and so forth, are said to be in three categories [imputational, other-powered, and thoroughly established natures], and from among them those said to be self-empty are in consideration of imputational and other-powered forms and so forth...

Similarly, with respect to the statement:

> Because the element of attributes is void, Bodhisattvas do not apprehend a prior limit. Because thusness, the limit of reality, and the inconceivable basic element are void, Bodhisattvas do not apprehend a prior limit.

you should also understand that although it is not void of itself, it is void of others, and through having become mindful again and again of this unique profound essential of quintessential instructions that also explain well the many occasions of non-establishment, purity, intensive purity, thorough purity, ceasedness, cessation, extinction, separation, intensive separation, purity, abandonment, and so forth, you will understand well:

- the meaning of the emptiness of its own entity and the emptiness of other entities
- the meaning of empty emptiness and non-empty emptiness
- the meaning of the emptiness of non-entities and the emptiness that is the [ultimate] nature of non-entities [that is, emptiness that is the ultimate nature opposite from non-entities]
- the mere emptiness of the phenomenon that is the object negated and the emptiness that has many synonyms such as basis of emptiness, noumenon, thusness, and so forth.

Concerning that, from among the three characters—imputational, other-powered, and thoroughly established:

1. Imputational characters[a] are all objects apprehended through mental superimposition:
    - all non-things—space and so forth
    - factors of the appearance of objects—the forms and so

[a] *kun brtags pa'i mtshan nyid, parikalpitalakṣaṇa.*

forth that appear to conceptual consciousnesses[a]
- the relationship of name and meaning—in which names are adhered to as meanings and meanings are mistaken as names
- external and internal, center and ends, big and small, good and bad, directions, time, and so forth.

2. Other-powered characters[b] are just consciousnesses to which there are appearances as the actualities of apprehended-object and apprehending-subject, because [such consciousnesses] appear through having come under the other-influence of the predispositions of ignorance.

3. The thoroughly established character[c] is self-illuminating self-cognition devoid of all proliferations. Noumenon,[d] element of attributes,[e] thusness,[f] and ultimate truth[g] are synonyms [of the thoroughly established character].

Regarding these [three characters], although the two—other-powered characters and imputational characters—are equally without true existence, are equally mistaken appearances, and are equally conventionalities[h] and falsities, the necessity to distinguish their characters individually is that imputational characters do not exist even conventionally and other-powered natures conventionally exist.[i] Since the thoroughly established character does not conventionally exist but ultimately exists, it truly exists.

---

[a] These are images of forms and so forth that are the appearing-objects (*snang yul*) of conceptual consciousnesses, called meaning-generalities (*don spyi, arthasāmānya*) in other contexts.

[b] *gzhan dbang gi mtshan nyid, paratantralakṣaṇa.*

[c] *yongs su grub pa'i mtshan nyid, pariniṣpannalakṣaṇa.*

[d] *chos nyid, dharmatā.*

[e] *chos dbyings, dharmadhātu.*

[f] *de bzhin nyid, tathatā.*

[g] *don dam bden pa, paramārthasatya.*

[h] *kun rdzob, saṃvṛti;* this could also be translated as "fraudulences."

[i] For Döl-bo-ba's description of imputational natures as "always not existing" and other-powered natures as "tentatively existent" see p. 87.

> Döl-bo-ba's *Mountain Doctrine* (233) summarizes presentations of the three natures as indicating that:
>
> - The basis of the emptiness of the imputational nature is other-powered natures.
> - The basis of the emptiness also of those [other-powered natures] is the thoroughly established nature.
> - A basis of the emptiness of that [thoroughly established nature] does not occur...
> - Both of the former two [that is, imputational natures and other-powered natures] are imputational natures.[a]
> - The basis of the emptiness of them is the ultimate.
> - A basis of the emptiness of that [ultimate] does not occur.

Similarly, imputational characters imputedly exist; other-powered characters substantially exist,[b] and although the thoroughly established character does not exist in either of those two ways, it exists without proliferations. Imputational characters are non-existent-empty; other-powered characters are existent-empty; and the thoroughly established character is the ultimate emptiness. The holy leader [Maitreya] says [in the *Ornament for the Great Vehicle Sūtras*]:[c]

> When one knows non-existent-emptiness
> And likewise existent-emptiness
> And the nature-emptiness,
> It is said that one knows emptiness.

> Döl-bo-ba's *Mountain Doctrine* (219-220): The imputational nature is empty in the sense of always not existing. Other-powered natures, although tentatively existent, are

---

[a] Imputational natures and other-powered natures are sometimes considered separately, and sometimes are treated as just imputational natures.

[b] For Döl-bo-ba's presentation of distinctions about substantial existence with respect to the three natures, see p. 75.

[c] XIV.34; Sanskrit in Lévi, *Mahāyāna Sūtrālaṃkāra*, 94:

*abhāvaśūnyatāṃ jñātvā tathābhāvasya śūnyatāṃ/ prakṛtyā śūnyatāṃ jñātvā śūnyajña iti kathyate//*

> empty in the sense of not existing in reality; those two are fabricated and adventitious. It is said that the noumenal thoroughly established nature exists because the emptiness that is the [ultimate] nature of non-entities [that is, the emptiness that is the ultimate nature opposite from non-entities]—due to being just the fundamental nature—is not empty of its own entity, and it is also said that it does not exist because of being empty even of other-powered natures.

Imputational characters are character-non-natures;[a] other-powered characters are production-non-natures;[b] and the thoroughly established character is the ultimate-non-nature.[c] [Vasubandhu's *The Thirty* says:][d]

---

[a] *mtshan nyid ngo bo nyid med pa, lakṣaṇaniḥsvabhāva.* Imputational characters are called character-non-natures because they lack the nature of existing by way of their own character, since they are only imputed and do not exist even conventionally.

[b] *skye ba ngo bo nyid med pa, utpattiniḥsvabhāva.* Other-powered characters are called production-non-natures because they lack the nature of being produced under their own power, since they arise in dependence upon causes and conditions.

[c] *don dam pa ngo bo nyid med pa, paramārthaniḥsvabhāva.* The thoroughly established character is called the ultimate-non-nature because it is the ultimate and lacks the nature of conventionalities.

[d] *sum cu pa'i tshig le'ur byas pa, triṃśikākārikā;* P5556, vol. 113, 233.3.3; stanza 23. Wonch'uk cites this in his *Extensive Commentary on the Sūtra Unraveling the Thought,* P5517, vol. 116, 130.4.8. The Sanskrit from Sylvain Lévi, *Vijñaptimātratāsiddhi / Deux traités de Vasubandhu: Viṃśatikā (La Vingtaine) et Triṃsikā (La Trentaine),* Bibliothèque de l'École des Hautes Études 245 (Paris: Libraire Ancienne Honoré Champion, 1925), 14, is:

> *trividhasya svabhāvasya trividhāṃ niḥsvabhāvatām /*
> *saṃdhāya sarvadharmāṇāṃ deśitā niḥsvabhāvatā //*

See also K. N. Chatterjee, *Vijñapti-Mātratā-Siddhi (with Sthiramati's Commentary)* (Varanasi, India; Kishor Vidya Niketan, 1980), 122; Thomas E. Wood, *Mind-Only: A Philosophical and Doctrinal Analysis of the Vijñānavāda,* Monographs of the Society for Asian and Comparative

In reliance on three aspects of non-nature
Of the three aspects of nature,
[Buddha] taught that all phenomena
Are natureless.

> Döl-b̄o-b̄a's *Mountain Doctrine* (401): Imputational natures are natureless in that they are do not exist by way of their own character; aside from being established as mere conventionalities, or as unreal conventionalities, they are not established even as conventional truths, or real conventionalities. Other-powered natures are natureless in that although they exist as entities conventionally produced from others, they do not exist as entities produced from themselves, and in reality they are not established at all. Because in that way those two are self-empty, their entities [that is, natures] do not exist. The basis of the non-existence of those two, the noumenal thoroughly established nature, is not without its own entity, but because it is the basis of the non-existence of the natures of conventional phenomena, which are other than it, it is the entity of the ultimate truth—the nature body or inherent body, natural clear light, natural innate pristine wisdom, natural purity, natural spontaneity, naturally abiding lineage.
>
> It is said that when you know the system of naturelessness in that way, you realize the center that has not fallen to an extreme of existence and non-existence, permanence and annihilation, and superimposition and deprecation, whereby you will not degenerate from the middle path.

In this system, all objects of knowledge are necessarily emptinesses[a] and are necessarily natureless.[a] Therefore, the assertion that

Philosophy 9 (Honolulu: University of Hawaii Press, 1991), 54; and Enga Teramoto, *Sthiramati's Triṃçikābhāṣyaṃ (Sum-cu-paḥi ḥGrel-pa): A Tibetan Text* (Kyoto: Association for Linguistic Study of Sacred Scriptures, 1933), 79.14.

[a] All conventionalities are self-emptinesses, and ultimates are other-emptinesses. Döl-b̄o-b̄a (*Mountain Doctrine,* 338) clearly states that the

all phenomena are emptinesses and that an emptiness of all phenomena does not exist is the system of other-emptiness;[b] there are

---

ultimate is an object of knowledge:

> Hence, those who propound that all objects of knowledge are limited to the two, existing as an effective thing and not existing as an effective thing (*dngos po yod med*), are reduced to only not having realized the ultimate mode of subsistence, since although it is an object of knowledge, it does not either exist as an effective thing or not exist as an effective thing. Consequently, it is also established as just a third category and the center or middle.

[a] All objects of knowledge are natureless in that, as stated just above, imputational characters are character-non-natures; other-powered characters are production-non-natures; and the thoroughly established character is the ultimate-non-nature.

[b] The two editions of Tāranātha's text have radically different readings of this line. There are four such conflicts (see also footnotes c on p. 92, f on p. 93, and a on p. 98) between the two editions likely due to variant readings of a contraction; it is possible that the Dzamthang edition is corrupt all four times but, to my mind, certainly in the final one.

> Smanrtsis Shesrig Dpemzod edition, 8a.7: *des na chos* ***thams cad*** *stong nyid dang/ chos* ***thams cad*** *stong nyid med par khas len pa gzhan stong lugs yin.* Therefore, the assertion that all phenomena are emptinesses and that an emptiness of all phenomena does not exist is the system of other-emptiness.

> Dzamthang edition, 8a.4: *des na chos* ***nyid*** *stong nyid dang/ chos* ***nyid*** *stong nyid med par khas len pa gzhan stong lugs yin.* Therefore, the assertion that the noumenon is emptiness and that an emptiness of the noumenon does not exist is the system of other-emptiness.

With regard to the first reading, how "all phenomena are emptinesses" is explained in the previous note about how all objects of knowledge are natureless; also, all conventional phenomena are self-emptinesses. It seems to me that in the statement "an emptiness of all phenomena does not exist" the term "all phenomena" (*chos thams cad*) includes both phenomena and noumenon (*chos dang chos nyid*), and since the noumenon is not empty of the noumenon, it cannot be said that the noumenon is empty of all phenomena; rather, it is empty of all conventional phenomena. In the same vein, it is not the case that all phenomena are empty of true or

internal contradictions in the system renowned a self-emptiness.[a]

ultimate existence, since the thoroughly established nature is not empty of true or ultimate existence.

Depending on how it used, sometimes the term "phenomena" includes the noumenon, and sometimes it does not, the latter being called "phenomena (*chos*) in the division of phenomena (*chos*) into phenomena (*chos*) and noumenon (*chos nyid*)." Döl-b̄o-b̄a (*Mountain Doctrine,* 404-405) uses the term in its more restrictive sense when addressing this same general issue:

> *Objection:* If [other-emptiness] is empty of all phenomena, it would even be empty of the noumenon because the noumenon is also included within all.
>
> *Answer:* An emptiness of all (*thams cad kyi stong pa*) does not occur because an emptiness of the noumenon does not occur. A basis of the emptiness of all phenomena (*chos thams cad kyi stong pa'i gzhi*) occurs; it is the noumenon. A basis empty of the noumenon (*chos nyid kyi stong pa'i gzhi*) does not occur because that is damaged by immeasurable, great, absurd consequences. Therefore, empty of all and empty of all phenomena are extremely different because the mode of subsistence is empty of phenomena but is not empty of the noumenon (*gnas lugs la chos kyis stong yang chos nyid kyis mi stong*). This also clears away the assertion that phenomena and noumenon are one entity and different isolates (*ngo bo gcig la ldog pa tha dad*) and the assertion that they are not at all different because those two are different in the sense of negating that they are the same entity (*ngo bo gcig pa bkag pa'i tha dad*).

With regard to the second reading, the noumenon is emptiness in that the noumenon is other-emptiness, since it is empty of conventionalities. However, an emptiness of the noumenon does not occur because the noumenon is the final nature of all phenomena. Döl-b̄o-b̄a frequently calls the noumenon "the basis of emptiness, the ultimate other-emptiness" (*stong gzhi don dam gzhan stong*), in that it is empty of conventionalities, or compounded phenomena, but it is not empty of itself and hence is non-empty emptiness (*mi stong ba'i stong nyid*).

[a] In Ge-luk, all phenomena, including the noumenon, are self-empty in that even emptiness, the noumenon, is empty of inherent existence. Hence, in Ge-luk "self-empty" does not mean that a phenomenon is empty of itself; rather, it means that a phenomenon is empty of its own

> Döl-b̄o-b̄a's *Mountain Doctrine* (213): Moreover, if everything were self-empty, then the body of attributes of release also would be self-empty, and if that is accepted, it also would be totally non-existent.

Therefore, the pure self-emptiness set forth by Buddha is that conventionalities abide as self-empty, and naturelessness also is these three [non-natures described above]. Hence, those propounding self-emptiness without error and the definitive Proponents of Naturelessness[a] are the Proponents of Other-Emptiness. That Bhāvaviveka, Buddhapālita, and so forth are renowned as Proponents of Self-Emptiness and Proponents of Naturelessness is a case of mainly taking what is renowned to the ordinary world.[b]

*Question:* If the thoroughly established character exists as truly established, does it have the three (production, abiding, and cessation), going and coming, change and reversal, direction and time, one and many, and so forth?

*Answer:* No, whatever has those necessarily is without true existence. The thoroughly established character is without production, without abiding, and without cessation; it is without going and without coming; it is not one and not many; it is not a cause and is not an effect; by way of its own nature it has abandoned definition, definiendum, and illustration; it is devoid of all directions and times; by way of its own nature it is not related with any conventional phenomena. Because it does not have any pieces to be separated off, it is partless. Because it is the noumenon of all phenomena,[c] it is omnipresent and all-pervasive.

---

inherent existence. However, if it meant that all phenomena are empty of themselves, then even the ultimate would not exist; this is likely the contradiction to which Tāranātha is referring.

a *ngo bo nyid med smra ba yin nges;* that is to say, those who actually are Proponents of Naturelessness and do not stray into asserting that the ultimate lacks true existence.

b They are actually Proponents of Other-Emptiness, who indeed know how to propound self-emptiness and naturelessness properly.

c *chos thams cad kyi chos nyid:* Smanrtsis Shesrig Dpemzod edition, 8b.6. The Dzamthang edition (8b.2) reads *chos nyid kyi chos nyid* "the noumenon of the noumenon." The noumenon is not empty of the

## *The Uncommon Meaning*

Maitreya's *Ornament for the Great Vehicle Sūtras* says:[a]

> Because thusness does not differ in all,
> And its state of having been purified
> Is the One-Gone-Thus,
> All transmigrating beings have its matrix.[b]

This means that thusness and One-Gone-Thus are one entity and that just this is the matrix-of-One-Gone-Thus. Matrix-of-One-Gone-Thus,[c] matrix-of-One-Gone-to-Bliss,[d] and Buddha-matrix[e] are equivalent. Although it resides equally in all phenomena[f]—Buddhas, sentient beings, and so forth—it resides in sentient beings in the manner of a matrix, and it resides in Buddhas in a manifest manner. Therefore, the ultimate Buddha itself exists like a matrix in the middle of the mental continuums of sentient beings, and consequently it is said that all sentient beings possess the matrix-of-One-Gone-Thus. This matrix-of-One-Gone-to-Bliss exists in sentient beings, and sentient beings' matrix-of-One-Gone-to-Bliss is also called the "naturally abiding lineage"[g] and "basic constituent."[a]

---

noumenon, but I wonder whether the frequent description of the noumenon as the basis of emptiness (*stong gzhi*) might provide an avenue for positing an emptiness of the noumenon, or noumenon of the noumenon.

[a] IX.37; W̄el-mang Ḡön-chok-gyel-tsen's *Blossoming Flower,* 122.1; Lévi, *Mahāyāna Sūtrālaṃkāra,* 40: *sarveṣāmaviśiṣṭāpi tathatā śuddhimāgatā/ tathāgatatvaṃ tasmācca tadgarbhāḥ sarvadehinaḥ//.*

[b] Döl-b̄o-b̄a (*Mountain Doctrine,* 82 and 247) cites this stanza twice, commenting that, "in consideration that the basal and resultant entities are the same in thusness, it is even said that the basal, or causal, continuum is the fruit continuum..." and, "That there is no one whose naturally abiding lineage is severed is extensively set forth in this very text."

[c] *de bzhin gshegs pa'i snying po, tathāgatagarbha.*

[d] *bde bar gzhegs pa'i snying po, sugatagarbha.*

[e] *sangs rgyas kyi snying po.*

[f] *chos thams cad la:* Smanrtsis Shesrig Dpemzod edition, 8b.6. The Dzamthang edition (8b.4) reads *chos nyid la,* "in the noumenon."

[g] *rang bzhin gnas rigs.*

*Question:* Therefore, since thusness does not reside in a Buddha in the manner of a matrix and a sentient being's thusness resides in the manner of a matrix, would thusness be twofold?

*Answer:* It is not. Buddha is thusness itself. Even when "Buddha" is explained as having the meaning of a person, to itself [thusness] is manifest, non-hidden; consequently, when the meaning of matrix is taken as "abiding and hidden within,"[b] the etymology of matrix as "hidden within" is not complete [in Buddha]. Although just that thusness of a Buddha abides in sentient beings, sentient beings do not perceive it from their own side, and hence it is a matrix that has the meaning of being hidden to sentient beings. [However] when matrix is explained as "immutability,"[c] even a Buddha has the Buddha-matrix. Therefore, this matrix-of-One-Gone-Thus is released from both effective things and non-things, due to which it is the actual uncompounded,[d] the ultimate uncompounded.[e]

Moreover, with respect to the secret uncommon mode of subsistence, there is no controversy over the fact that a Buddha's element of attributes exists as an entity of all Buddha-qualities, and just it is not divisible from sentient beings' element of attributes. Consequently, what unsuitability is there in the matrix-of-One-Gone-to-Bliss in the continuums of sentient beings also abiding as an entity of all Buddha-qualities! Therefore, Maitreya's *Sublime Continuum of the Great Vehicle* says:[f]

> [The uncontaminated basic element, the naturally] luminous [body of attributes,] is not compounded [from causes and conditions]
> And permeates undifferentiably [as the nature of all sentient beings];
> It [primordially and spontaneously] just possesses all of the [unlimited] Buddha-attributes

a *khams, dhātu.*

b *khong na gnas pa dang sbas pa.*

c *mi 'gyur ba.*

d *'dus ma byas dngos.*

e *don dam pa'i 'dus ma byas.*

f II.5; brackets are from Döl-b̄o-b̄a's *Rays of the Sun,* 113.3ff.

[Of the powers and so forth] beyond the [count of] sands of the Ganges.

> Döl-b̄o-b̄a's *Mountain Doctrine* (99): This matrix-of-One-Gone-Thus itself, the naturally luminous and uncompounded noumenon, is endowed undifferentiably with the inseparable qualities of Buddhahood passed beyond the count of the grains of sands of the banks of the Ganges.

Since it says that [the matrix-of-One-Gone-to-Bliss in the continuums of sentient beings] is endowed with all the qualities that are uncompounded entities, it has all the ultimate Buddha-qualities.

Therefore, the pristine wisdom of the element of attributes necessarily is only an ultimate truth; although the other four pristine wisdoms are mainly the primordially abiding ultimate, each in a minor way has conventional portions that are newly attained through having cultivated the path.

> Döl-b̄o-b̄a's *Mountain Doctrine* (456-457): The pristine wisdom of the pure element of attributes is only ultimate, whereas there are compounded and uncompounded [types] with regard to the four—the mirror-like wisdom and so forth—whereby it should be known that there are conventional [ones] and there are also ultimate [ones].

The ten powers, four fearlessnesses, and so forth also are similar to those [four pristine wisdoms in mainly being the primordially abiding ultimate, but each in a minor way has conventional parts that are newly attained through having cultivated the path]. The qualities of exalted body (the marks, the beauties, and so forth) and the qualities of exalted speech (the sixty branches [of vocalization] and so forth) each equally has conventional and ultimate portions. Likewise, the nature body is only ultimate; the body of attributes is mostly ultimate; the two, the complete enjoyment body and emanation bodies, have equal portions when a division of actual and imputed types is not made; moreover, the appearances of exalted activities in others' perspectives are conventional, whereas the pristine wisdom of capable power[a] is ultimate.

---

[a] Smanrtsis Shesrig Dpemzod edition, 10a.2: *nus mthu'i ye shes;* Dzam-

Hence, all exalted body, pristine wisdom, qualities, and activities that are included within the ultimate abide primordially in the matrix-of-One-Gone-Thus. When a person is Buddhafied, those are not newly attained and are merely separated from defilements obscuring them, but those that are conventional are newly attained. In past Buddhas and in future Buddhas those that are ultimate are one entity, and even those that are conventional are indivisible in nature upon attaining Buddhahood and thereafter but at the point of attainment are different; hence, they are unpredicable as either the same or different.[a]

Therefore, newly attained effects that are to be produced through cultivating the path are produced effects, due to which they do not truly exist, whereas the primordially abiding Buddha is merely separated from the covering over that Buddha through cultivating the path, due to which it is called a "separative effect,"[b] and the path also is called a "cause of its separation."[c]

> Döl-b̄o-b̄a's *Mountain Doctrine* (426-428): Thus, it is said that:
>
> - separative effects, the body of attributes, are immutable thoroughly established natures, and separative qualities—the powers and so forth—are complete in the body of thusness
> - produced effects, form bodies, are undistorted thoroughly established natures, and produced qualities—the marks and so forth—exist in those having correct pristine wisdom.
>
> These [points] clear away the assertion by some that even the body of attributes is a produced effect, a conventionality, and the assertion by others that even form bodies are separative effects, ultimates...Likewise, the assertion by

---

thang edition, 9b.3 misreads *nus mthus ye shes.*

[a] They are the same from one perspective and different from another perspective and thus inexpressible as either.

[b] *bral 'bras.*

[c] *de'i bral rgyu.*

> some that even the body of attributes does not exist in sentient beings from the beginning and the assertion by others that even form bodies exist in sentient beings from the beginning are very mistaken because [Maitreya's *Sublime Continuum of the Great Vehicle*] says at length,[a] "Like a [great] treasure [that naturally remains under the ground—not newly achieved through striving and exertion and containing inexhaustible resources—]and like a fruit tree [that gradually grows in a grove by way of being achieved through striving and exertion]," and so forth.

These are merely imputed cause and effect, not actual cause and effect. This separative effect also is not an analytical separation[b] described in *Manifest Knowledge:* "Separation is a mental extinguishment." Rather, it is an ultimate separative effect and an ultimate true cessation in accordance with the statement in the *Questions of King Dhāraṇīshvara Sūtra,*[c] "Since it is primordially extinguished, it is called 'extinguishment.'"

*Objection:* Since obstructions are abandoned through the power of the path, this would be equivalent to extinguishment by the mind.

*Answer:* It is not that obstructions are abandoned from the side of the element of attributes; they are abandoned from the side of the person. Hence, persons who are enlightened get the mere designation, "They have attained a separation that is an extinguishment." However, since the element of attributes is primordially unpolluted by defilements, it is not a new extinguishment by the mind.

Therefore, the matrix-of-One-Gone-to-Bliss—the non-dual

---

[a] I.149a; brackets are from Döl-b̄o-b̄a's *Rays of the Sun,* 96.2ff.

[b] *so sor brtags 'gog.*

[c] P814, vol. 32. D̄zong-ka-b̄a cites this in his *Extensive Explanation of (Chandrakīrti's) "Supplement to (Nāgārjuna's) 'Treatise on the Middle'": Illumination of the Thought* (*dbu ma la 'jug pa'i rgya cher bshad pa dgongs pa rab gsal;* P6143, vol. 154) as:

> Extinction [in this case] is not [caused] by means of an antidote.
> It is so called because of primordial extinction.

pristine wisdom pervading all phenomena[a] equally—is adorned with all ultimate Buddha-qualities and is devoid of all proliferations. Just this which is endowed with all aspects of pristine wisdom but is devoid of all proliferations is the great immutable thoroughly established nature.[b] Only this is the undistorted mode of subsistence and is an object of experience by the unmistaken pristine wisdom of Superiors; hence, it is truly established, and because it is immutable, it is permanent, stable, and everlasting.[c] This matrix-of-One-Gone-to-Bliss that abides in the manner of possessing the qualities of the marks and the beauties and so forth is mentioned in all tantra sets of secret mantra by way of many synonyms.

> Döl-b̄o-b̄a's *Mountain Doctrine* (271-272):[d] These [texts] call "great seal" and "emptiness endowed with supreme aspects" just that undifferentiable element of attributes and self-arisen pristine wisdom, having a nature of:
>
> - the final definitive phallic bliss
> - selfless goddess
> - perfection of wisdom goddess
> - the letter *A*
> - lotus
> - thusness
> - emptiness
> - Vajrayoginī
> - lady lineage holder
>
> and so forth, and that also is the profound emptiness, which is not self-empty. Moreover, even these exalted sources speak of:
>
> - the final great seal of undifferentiable basis and fruit
> - great mother

[a] The Smanrtsis Shesrig Dpemzod edition (10b.3) reads *chos* ***thams cad;*** the Dzamthang edition (10a.4) misreads *chos* ***nyid.***

[b] *'gyur med yongs grub chen po.*

[c] *rtag brtan ther zug.*

[d] Döl-b̄o-b̄a gives long lists of synonyms throughout *Mountain Doctrine;* this is a sample.

- lady selflessness
- letter *A*
- lotus
- innate body or joy
- maṇḍala
- five pristine wisdoms
- thusness
- Vajrayoginī
- lady lineage holder

in consideration of:

- the basis empty of all phenomena
- noumenon
- ultimate truth
- matrix-of-One-Gone-to-Bliss having a nature of all inseparable qualities
- Buddha-nature
- thusness
- self of pure self
- emptiness that is the [ultimate] nature of non-entities [that is, emptiness that is the ultimate nature opposite from non-entities].

That thoroughly established nature is not polluted by, in brief, any appearing and consensual phenomena,[a] whether these are called "conventionalities"[b] or "apprehended-object and apprehending-subject"[c] or "mistaken appearances."[d] Moreover, with respect to this non-pollution, it is not that [conventionalities and the element of attributes] exist individually and separately, with conventionalities existing in fact[e] but unable to pollute the element of attributes. Rather, because conventionalities are only mistaken appearances, they, like the horns of a rabbit, are not established in the mode of

---

[a] *snang grags kyi chos,* "phenomena appearing and renowned [to all]."

[b] *kun rdzob.*

[c] *gzung 'dzin.*

[d] *'khrul ba'i snang ba.*

[e] *dngos gnas la yod pa.*

subsistence.

> Döl-bo-ba's *Mountain Doctrine* (537): Therefore, these mistaken karmic appearances of sentient beings are the private phenomena just of sentient beings; they utterly do not occur in the mode of subsistence, like the horns of a rabbit, the child of a barren woman, a sky-flower, and so forth. Consequently, they are not established even as mere appearances to a consciousness of the mode of subsistence, and appearing in the perspective of mistake does not fulfill the role of appearing in the mode of subsistence. In consideration of these, it is again and again said in many formats that all phenomena are not observed, non-appearing, unapprehendable, and so forth.

> Döl-bo-ba's *Mountain Doctrine* (527): [Vasubandhu's] *Commentary on the Extensive and Middling Mothers* and so forth say that because in the mode of subsistence these imputational three realms are utterly non-existent like the horns of a rabbit, they do not appear to a consciousness of the mode of subsistence, just as the horns of a rabbit do not appear to an unmistaken consciousness.

> Döl-bo-ba's *Mountain Doctrine* (535-536): That the noumenon exists in the mode of subsistence and that phenomena do not exist in the mode of subsistence are set forth in many elevated, pure scriptural systems such as Maitreya's *Differentiation of Phenomena and Noumenon* and so forth. If you are skilled in the thought of similar, extensive statements of existing and not existing in the mode of subsistence such as:
>
> - the ultimate exists, but the conventional does not exist
> - nirvāṇa exists, but cyclic existence does not exist
> - true cessation exists, but the other three truths do not exist
> - the noumenal thoroughly established nature exists, but the other natures do not exist
> - thusness exists, but other phenomena do not exist

- external and internal adventitious defilements do not exist, but the alternative supreme matrix-of-One-Gone-to-Bliss exists,

you will know them within differentiating well existence and non-existence.

Hence [the thoroughly established nature] is not polluted in the sense that the causes of pollution do not exist.[a]

> Döl-b̄o-b̄a's *Mountain Doctrine* (331): Since the ultimate's own entity is even very established, it is not non-existent, and imputational things, which are other than that, do not arise or do not exist.

Therefore, the thoroughly established nature, the matrix-of-One-Gone-to-Bliss, is never empty of its own entity but is primordially empty of others, that is, conventionalities. Hence, the thoroughly established nature, the ultimate truth, is other-empty, not self-empty.[b] Consequently, conventionalities, in addition to being

---

[a] *gos rgyu med nas ma gos pa yin.*

[b] This is Döl-b̄o-b̄a's main theme in *Mountain Doctrine,* as for instance, when he says (212):

> Using the example of a hailstone becoming non-existent upon melting, Aṅgulimāla teaches that all afflicted and non-virtuous phenomena are empty; this teaches that all that are included among mundane conventional truths are empty of themselves and of [their own] entities. Using the example of a *vaiḍūrya* jewel, which does not become non-existent upon melting, he teaches that the final liberation, Buddhahood, is not empty. This teaches that the ultimate supramundane truth, the body of attributes, is not empty of its own entity. Using the example of an empty home, an empty vase, and an empty river, he teaches an emptiness of all defects; this teaches that the final liberation is other-emptiness. All descriptions of non-emptiness—"liberation is not empty in all respects," "a Supramundane Victor is not empty," "non-empty phenomena are other," and so forth—mean that the ultimate noumenon is not itself empty of itself. The very many statements in other sūtras and tantras of "is not empty" and "non-empty" also are similar.

empty of others' entities, are also empty of their own entities, and the ultimate is empty of only others' entities. Due to this, those who propound this mode are the Other-Empty Middle.[a]

Concerning this, in order to overcome any and all attachments to the phenomena of cyclic existence, you should meditatively cultivate the intention definitely to leave cyclic existence, meditating on impermanence and suffering. Also, you should abandon taking to mind your own welfare[b] and inculcate in your continuum the altruistic intention to become enlightened. In order to abandon coarse attachments to conventionalities, you should delineate and then meditate on conventionalities as without true existence. In order also to abandon subtle attachments, you should meditatively cultivate non-conceptuality, withdrawing conceptuality of the conventional into the basic element. Through those, you will come to the non-conceptual matrix-of-One-Gone-to-Bliss and gradually meet its face. Hence, all whatsoever meditative cultivations of the path are for the sake of encountering the thoroughly established nature.

## III. Clearing Away Extremes Imputed by Others

You should know about this from my *Ornament of the Other-Empty Middle*,[c] and also I will explain this at length elsewhere. However, let us give the essence in brief.

*Others say:* In the *Descent into Laṅkā Sūtra*, [Mahāmati] asks, "If there is a One-Gone-to-Bliss endowed with the marks and beauties [of a Buddha], would it not be the same as the self of [non-Buddhist] Forders?" And in answer, [Buddha] says, "It is not the same because of being emptiness." Hence, the matrix-of-One-Gone-to-Bliss is without true existence, and if it had the marks, beauties, and so forth [of a Buddha], this would be the system of Forders, whereby non-establishment as anything, like space, is what is called the "matrix-of-One-Gone-to-Bliss."

Döl-b̄o-b̄a's *Mountain Doctrine* (117-118) cites the passage

---

a *gzhan stong dbu ma.*

b *rang don yid byed.*

c *gzhan stong dbu ma'i rgyan.*

in the *Descent into Laṅkā Sūtra:*[a]

Mahāmati said, "The matrix-of-One-Gone-Thus taught in other sūtras spoken by the Supramundane Victor was said by the Supramundane Victor to be naturally radiant, pure, and thus from the beginning just pure. The matrix-of-One-Gone-Thus is said to possess the thirty-two marks [of a Buddha] and to exist in the bodies of all sentient beings.

"The Supramundane Victor said that like a precious gem wrapped in a dirty cloth, the matrix-of-One-Gone-Thus is wrapped in the cloth of the aggregates, constituents, and sense-spheres, overwhelmed by the force of desire, hatred, and ignorance, and dirtied with the defilements of conceptuality.

"Since this which is dirtied with the defilements of conceptuality was said to be permanent, stable, and everlasting, Supramundane Victor, how is this propounding of a matrix-of-One-Gone-Thus not like the [non-Buddhist] Forders' propounding of a self? Supramundane Victor, the Forders teach and propound a self that is permanent, the agent, without qualities, pervasive, and non-perishing."

The Supramundane Victor said, "Mahāmati, my teaching of a matrix-of-One-Gone-Thus is not like the Forders' propounding of a self. O Mahāmati, the completely perfect Buddhas, Ones-Gone-Thus, Foe Destroyers, teach a matrix-of-One-Gone-Thus for the meaning of the words 'emptiness,' 'limit of reality,' 'nirvāṇa,' 'no

---

[a] P775, vol. 29, 39.5.5ff., chapter 2; Daisetz Teitaro Suzuki, trans., *The Lankavatara Sutra* (London: Routledge and Kegan Paul, 1932), 68-70. The passage up through "How could those with thoughts fallen into incorrect views conceiving of self come to be endowed with thought abiding in the spheres of the three liberations and come to be quickly, manifestly, and completely purified in unsurpassed complete perfect enlightenment," is quoted in Chandrakīrti's *Commentary on the "Supplement"* (P5263, vol. 98, 136.1.4ff), commenting on VI.95; Louis de La Vallée Poussin, *Madhyamakāvatāra par Candrakīrti,* Bibliotheca Buddhica 9 (Osnabrück, Germany: Biblio Verlag, 1970), 251-252; Jñānavajra's commentary is P5520, vol. 107, 246.4.4.

production,' 'signlessness,' 'wishlessness,' and so forth. So that children might avoid the fear of selflessness, they teach through the means of a matrix-of-One-Gone-Thus the state of non-conceptuality, the object [of wisdom] free from appearances.

"Mahāmati, future and present Bodhisattvas—great beings—should not adhere to this as a self. Mahāmati, for example, potters make a variety of vessels out of one mass of clay particles with their hands, manual skill, a rod, water, string, and mental dexterity. Mahāmati, similarly the Ones-Gone-Thus also teach the selflessness of phenomena that is an absence of all conceptual signs. Through various [techniques] endowed with wisdom and skill in means—whether they teach it as the matrix-of-One-Gone-Thus or as selflessness—they, like a potter, teach with various formats of words and letters.

"Therefore, Mahāmati, the teaching of the matrix-of-One-Gone-Thus is not like the teaching propounding a self for Forders. Mahāmati, in order to lead Forders who are attached to propounding self, the Ones-Gone-Thus teach the matrix-of-One-Gone-Thus through the teaching of a matrix-of-One-Gone-Thus. Thinking, 'How could those with thoughts fallen into incorrect views conceiving of self come to be endowed with thought abiding in the spheres of the three liberations and come to be quickly, manifestly, and completely purified in unsurpassed complete perfect enlightenment?' Mahāmati, for their sake the Ones-Gone-Thus, Foe Destroyers, completely perfect Buddhas, teach the matrix-of-One-Gone-Thus. Consequently, that is not the same as propounding the self of Forders. Therefore, Mahāmati, in order to overcome the view of Forders, they cause them to engage the matrix-of-One-Gone-Thus, selflessness. It is this way: this teaching of the emptiness of phenomena, non-production, non-dualism, and absence of inherent nature is the unsurpassed tenet of Bodhisattvas. Through thoroughly apprehending this teaching of the profound doctrine, one thoroughly apprehends all sūtras of the Great Vehicle."

*Answer:* The identification of all whatsoever emptinesses as meaning an absence of true existence and aspectless mere non-establishment as anything is the fault of a mind adhering to one's own bad tenets. The [*Descent into Laṅkā*] *Sūtra* itself states—as the reason for non-similarity with the Forders—that [the matrix-of-One-Gone-to-Bliss] is emptiness; it does not state that it is without the marks and beauties [of a Buddha]. Therefore, the statement that it explains that a matrix-of-One-Gone-to-Bliss having the complete luminous marks and beauties requires interpretation is reduced to mere deception of the world with lies.

Also, saying that that assertion that the matrix is permanent is the system of [non-Buddhist] Forders is reduced to being a refutation of sūtras on the matrix. Moreover, it is not feasible to assert that the meaning of permanence is the permanence of a continuum[a] because all of cyclic existence and of apprehended-object and apprehending-subject have a mere permanence of continuum and because if mere permanence of continuum served as permanence, then even all compounded things would be permanent.

> Döl-b̄o-b̄a's *Mountain Doctrine* (161-162): Furthermore, the superior presence Lokeshvara [that is, Kalkī Puṇḍarīka] says that the pristine wisdom of thusness transcends momentariness: "This says that the pristine wisdom devoid of single or plural moments is the thusness of Conquerors"; and, moreover, the statements by the Conqueror, the holy protector Maitreya:
>
> - that the noumenon, the nature body, is a permanent nature:
>
>   > Those are asserted as permanent due to the continuity
>   > Of being the nature and having an uninterrupted continuum.
>
> - and that the final Buddha is uncompounded: "[Because of having a nature without the compounded

a "Permanence of a continuum" means that a continuum of impermanent moments goes on forever.

> attributes of production, abiding, and disintegration in the beginning, middle, and end, Buddha] is uncompounded, and [because of having an essence of the body of attributes in which the entirety of striving and exertion such as proliferations of body and speech, mental conceptuality, and so forth are pacified, exalted activities are] spontaneous,"[a]

and so forth, are in consideration that it is devoid of momentariness. Hence, those who assert that:

- all statements that the body of attributes or pristine wisdom are permanent are in consideration that their continuum is permanent and [the body of attributes or pristine wisdom actually] is impermanent due to being momentary
- and all statements that Buddha or pristine wisdom is uncompounded are in consideration that they are not compounded by actions and afflictive emotions

are reduced to merely not realizing these meanings of great import because of just not seeing these profound scriptures.

*Objection:* Because initially it is defiled and later becomes undefiled, it is impermanent.

*Answer:* From the side of the element of attributes, it is not initially defiled and also does not later become undefiled. However, its becoming defiled and undefiled is relative to a person's continuum; hence, the noumenon does not come to change in state due to changes in the states of sentient beings.

> Döl-b̄o-b̄a's *Mountain Doctrine* (405-406):
>
> *Objection:* Thusness released from the coverings of afflictive emotions is not the matrix-of-One-Gone-to-Bliss because it is said:
>
> Supramundane Victor, just this body of attributes not

---

[a] *Sublime Continuum* I.5a; brackets are from Döl-b̄o-b̄a's *Rays of the Sun,* 37.6.

released from the coverings of afflictive emotions is called the matrix-of-One-Gone-Thus.

*Answer:* Since some think this, let me explain. Although thusness residing pervasively during three phases of each individual person is said to be impure, impure-pure, and very pure, thusness—like space pervading an area whether or not there are groups of clouds—is neither one-pointedly pure nor one-pointedly impure because it resides pervading all persons, whether they have defilements or not. Consequently, due to persons, that which is thusness itself, residing together with defilement in some, resides without defilement in some [others], but there are no divisions in thusness, like space in which there are and are not clouds. In consideration of this:

- The *Excellent Golden Light Sūtra* says that the entity itself of a One-Gone-Thus and the matrix-of-One-Gone-Thus are equivalent.
- The *Mahāparinirvāṇa Sūtra* and so forth say that Buddha-nature, natural nirvāṇa, and basic element of self are synonyms.
- The *Descent into Laṅkā Sūtra* also says that matrix-of-One-Gone-to-Bliss, noumenon, and thoroughly established nature are synonyms.
- The *Expression of Mañjushrī's Ultimate Names Tantra* also says that vajra matrix, matrix of all Buddhas, and matrix of all Ones-Gone-Thus are synonyms of the ultimate.
- The *Matrix-of-One-Gone-Thus Sūtra* also says that Conqueror, matrix-of-One-Gone-Thus, self-arisen Buddha, Buddha ground, inexhaustible noumenon, treasure of attributes, noumenon of One-Gone-Thus, body of One-Gone-to-Bliss, body of a Conqueror set in equipoise, lineage of One-Gone-Thus, noumenon, precious pristine wisdom of One-Gone-Thus, nature, and pristine wisdom of Buddha are synonymous with matrix-of-One-Gone-to-Bliss.
- Maitreya's *Sublime Continuum of the Great Vehicle* and

> Asaṅga's commentary say that body of attributes, One-Gone-Thus, ultimate truth, and great nirvāṇa are synonymous with matrix-of-One-Gone-to-Bliss.

And others also say such at length. Hence, there is no fault in saying that [thusness and matrix-of-One-Gone-to-Bliss] are equivalent and synonymous.

*Objection:* It is not feasible for the pristine wisdom of a Buddha to exist in the continuums of sentient beings.

*Answer:* This directly contradicts the statement, "Since the Buddha-pristine-wisdom permeates the groups of sentient beings..."

Döl-b̄o-b̄a's *Mountain Doctrine* (185-187):

*Objection:* If the ultimate Buddha intrinsically exists in all sentient beings, then they intrinsically would have final abandonment [of defilements] and have final realization [of the truth].

*Answer:* This must be taught upon making a distinction. Hence, there are two types of abandonment—abandonment of all defilements that is their primordial absence of inherent establishment and extinguishment of adventitious defilements upon their being overcome by antidotes. Concerning those, the first is complete within the noumenon because of containing the entire meaning of:

> Extinguishment is not extinguishment by antidotes.
> Because of being extinguished from before, it is indicated as extinguishment...

and, "At all times devoid of all obstructions," and so forth, and because it is beyond the phenomena of consciousness, and because it is definitely released from all obstructions, and because of utterly having abandoned afflictive emotions, secondary afflictive emotions, and thorough afflictions as well as their predispositions, and because of the absence of dust, dustlessness, absence of defilements, abandonment of faults, and flawlessness. Hence, natural abandonment is primordially complete in the ultimate noumenal Buddha because the noumenon is the One-Gone-Thus primordially released and because of being the Buddha prior to all Buddhas.

Although the second abandonment [that is, the extinguishment of adventitious defilements upon being overcome by antidotes] does not exist in sentient beings who have not cultivated the path, this does not involve a fault in our tenets, because it is not asserted that all sentient beings are Buddhas or have attained Buddhahood and because it is not asserted that conventional Buddhahood exists in all sentient beings.

Similarly, there are also two types of Buddha-realization, the self-arisen pristine wisdom that is the primordial realization of the noumenon—knowing itself by itself—and the other-arisen pristine wisdom that is realization produced from having cultivated the profound path. The first is complete within the noumenon...Hence, natural fundamental abandonment and realization are complete in the ultimate noumenon...Therefore, since the first type of realization [self-arisen pristine wisdom that is primordial realization of the noumenon] is indivisibly complete in the noumenon, it is the case that where that noumenon exists, this realization also exists. Although the second type of realization [which is produced from having cultivated the profound path] is not complete in sentient beings who have not entered the path and although they have not directly realized selflessness, this does not involve a fault in our tenets; the reasons are as before.

*Objection:* It is not feasible for Buddha-qualities to exist in the continuums of sentient beings; for example, if the power of knowing sources and non-sources [that is, direct knowledge of cause and effect][a] existed in the continuums of sentient beings, sentient beings absurdly would understand all sources and non-sources.

---

[a] Brackets from Jeffrey Hopkins, *Meditation on Emptiness* (London: Wisdom Publications, 1983; rev. ed., Boston, Mass.: Wisdom Publications, 1996), 208.

*Answer:* This also is not correct, because we do not assert that whatever is [in] the continuums of sentient beings is a Buddha. And, if such necessarily follows due to the fact that Buddha and Buddha-qualities dwell in the continuums of sentient beings, then would it necessarily follow that, when a Buddha resides on a throne, even the throne would know all objects of knowledge?

> Döl-b̄o-b̄a's *Mountain Doctrine* (188): Therefore, very many distorted challenges such as, "If Buddha exists in sentient beings, all karmas, afflictive emotions, and sufferings would not exist," and so forth, and "Sentient beings would realize all knowables," and so forth are babble by those who do not know the difference between existence [or presence] and being such and such. This is because existence, [that is, presence] does not establish being such and such. If it did, then since explanations exist in humans, are humans explanations?[a]

Therefore, how could the eight collections of consciousness in the continuums of sentient beings be Buddha! Even the Buddha residing there does not reside in the manner of conventional support and that which is supported but resides there in the manner of being the ultimate noumenon [of the eight collections of consciousness].

At this point, let us speak a little about important vocabulary.[b] With regard to the three stages of the wheels of doctrine, the first is the wheel of doctrine of the four truths; the middle one is the wheel of doctrine of no character; the final one is the wheel of doctrine of good differentiation. The first is the Lesser Vehicle sūtras, the scriptural collections spoken for Hearers. Although the middle one is, so to speak, the root sūtras of the Great Vehicle, the intended meaning[c] is hidden.[d] The final wheel of doctrine is, so to speak, its [that

---

[a] Also cited earlier at p. 77.

[b] *brda chad.*

[c] Dzamthang edition, 11b.6: *dgongs don* (intended meaning/ meaning of its thought); Smanrtsis Shesrig Dpemzod edition, 12a.7: *dgos don* (purpose and meaning).

[d] *gab pa.*

is, the middle wheel's] explanatory tantra;[a] it teaches the definitive meaning very clearly.

> Döl-b̄o-b̄a's *Mountain Doctrine* (207): By reason of teaching unclearly [in the middle wheel], clearly [in the third wheel], and very clearly [in tantra], there are great and also very great differences of being obscured, not obscured, and so forth with respect to the meaning of those. Therefore, even the statements of being surpassable or unsurpassable, affording an opportunity [for refutation] or not affording an opportunity, and so forth are due to differences in those texts with respect to whether the final profound meaning is unclear and incomplete or clear and complete, and so forth, and are not due to the entity of the meaning.

From among the three natures—imputational, other-powered, and thoroughly established:

1. Imputational natures are twofold, apprehended imputational natures[b] and apprehender imputational natures.[c]
2. Other-powered natures are twofold, impure other-powered natures[d] and pure other-powered natures.[e]
3. Thoroughly established natures are twofold, immutable thoroughly established natures[f] and undistorted thoroughly established natures.[g]

From among these, actual imputational natures are the apprehended ones,[h] and actual thoroughly established natures are the

---

a *bshad rgyud.*

b *gzung ba'i kun brtags.*

c *'dzin pa'i kun brtags.*

d *ma dag pa'i gzhan dbang.*

e *dag pa'i gzhan dbang.*

f *'gyur med yongs grub.*

g *phyin ci ma log pa'i yongs grub.*

h The objects that are imputed, or imagined, to exist whereas they do not are the actual imputational natures, whereas, as Tāranātha says below, the consciousnesses imagining these non-existents are other-powered natures.

immutable ones and not the undistorted ones that are one entity with the immutable.

> Döl-b̄o-b̄a's *Mountain Doctrine* (425-427): Concerning this, the two exalted bodies are the ultimate body of attributes and the conventional form body—the sources of the fulfillment of one's own and others' welfare [respectively. Maitreya's *Sublime Continuum of the Great Vehicle*[a] says]...that:
>
> - separative effects, the body of attributes, are immutable thoroughly established natures, and separative qualities—the powers and so forth—are complete in the body of thusness
> - produced effects, form bodies, are undistorted thoroughly established natures, and produced qualities—the marks and so forth—exist in those having correct pristine wisdom.
>
> These [points] clear away the assertion by some that even the body of attributes is a produced effect, a conventionality, and the assertion by others that even form bodies are separative effects, ultimates.

Undistorted thoroughly established natures are included in pure other-powered natures.

> Döl-b̄o-b̄a's *Mountain Doctrine* (456): The undistorted thoroughly established nature—described as compounded—and the five pristine wisdoms delineated in Maitreya's *Ornament for the Great Vehicle Sūtras* are equivalent.[b]

Apprehender imputational natures and other-powered natures are one entity. When analyzed with reasoning, actual other-powered natures are included in imputational natures, and the mode of sub-

---

[a] III.1-3.

[b] Döl-b̄o-b̄a (*Mountain Doctrine,* 456) calls the undistorted thoroughly established nature compounded but he does not explicitly use the term "pure other-powered natures" in this text.

sistence that is their noumenon is the thoroughly established nature. Hence, all phenomena are included in the two, imputational natures and thoroughly established natures.

> Döl-b̄o-b̄a's *Mountain Doctrine* (232-233): Even in many various textual systems of the Great Middle, such as [Vasubandhu's] *Commentary on the One Hundred Thousand Stanza, Twenty-Five Thousand Stanza, and Eighteen Thousand Stanza Perfection of Wisdom Sūtras,* [Vasubandhu's] *Commentary on the One Hundred Thousand Perfection of Wisdom Sūtra,* and so forth presentations of the three natures are set forth saying that:
>
> - The basis of the emptiness of the imputational nature is other-powered natures.
> - Furthermore, the basis of the emptiness of those [other-powered natures] is the thoroughly established nature.
> - A basis of the emptiness of that [thoroughly established nature] does not occur.
>
> and also say that:
>
> - Both of the former two [that is, imputational natures and other-powered natures] are imputational natures.
> - The basis of the emptiness of them is the ultimate.
> - A basis of the emptiness of that [ultimate] does not occur.

The divisions of three characters [imputational, other-powered, and thoroughly established] or the two classes of the conventional associated with consciousness and of the ultimate, pristine wisdom, are posited with respect to all phenomena of cyclic existence and nirvāṇa.

> Regarding the six perfections Döl-b̄o-b̄a's *Mountain Doctrine* (323-324) says: Similarly, if you know the divisions of the three natures and the two truths with regard to the perfections of giving and so forth, you will not be obscured with respect to the Subduer's word. Concerning this, the perfections included among other-powered natures and

> true paths that are bases empty of imputational natures are conventional compounded phenomena and, therefore, are not established in the dispositional mode of subsistence. The perfections of giving and so forth that are bases primordially pure of those [imputational natures and conventional compounded phenomena] and are included in the noumenal thoroughly established nature are said to be just deities of ultimate pristine wisdom such as the ten shaktis, the ten lady sky-travelers, and so forth. And moreover, those are said to be the final ten seals [that is, consorts]—six, three, and one. Therefore, you should know that the meaning of pure and thoroughly pure noumenal perfections of giving and so forth is that they are naturally and spontaneously established deities.

This being so, since conventionalities such as forms, sounds, odors, tastes, and so forth are in the class of consciousness, they are without true existence, and since noumenal forms, sounds, and so forth[a] are in the class of pristine wisdom, they are truly established.

> Döl-b̄o-b̄a's *Mountain Doctrine* (316): In that way thusness, the basis of emptiness, having many synonyms is the basis primordially empty and void of all adventitious phenomena and is the pure basis. Hence, primordially pure phenomena ranging from forms through omniscience are noumenal thoroughly established forms and so forth and also forms and so on passed beyond the three realms and the three times.

Also, the class of conventionalities is multifarious,[b] and ultimate phenomena are without the fallacies of combinations of contradictions.

> Döl-b̄o-b̄a's *Mountain Doctrine* (346):[c] Similarly, that:

---

[a] *chos nyid kyi gzugs sgra sogs.*

[b] *tha dad.*

[c] For this frequent theme in *Mountain Doctrine* see its index under "contradictions, combination of."

- a non-fallacious combination of contradictories does not occur
- a third category does not occur with regard to direct contradictories [that is, with respect to dichotomies]
- objects of knowledge are limited to the two, effective thing and non-thing

and so forth are in terms of conventionalities, but ultimate truths are not included in any of those.

This also was written by the one called Tāranātha at the hermitage of Chö-lung Jang-d̄zay[a] upon requests by certain seekers.

Good luck.

Corrected once.[b]

---

a *chos lung byang rtse/chos lung byang chub rtse mo; chos lung* is a place in *gtsang rong; byang chub rtse mo* is a monastery.

b *gcig zhus.*

# *Twenty-one Differences Regarding the Profound Meaning*

by Tāranātha

Contradictions in perspective among those
Seeing the profound do not occur, I think,
But they speak differently due to perceiving
Different trainees and needs.

Here although the two—the leader of doctrine, the Great Omniscient One Endowed with the Four Reliances [Döl-b̄o-b̄a S̄hay-rap-gyel-tsen], and the great paṇḍita, the Conqueror Shākya Chok-den—are of one essential regarding the view and meditation of the other-empty middle,[a] I will identify many minor different tenets in their incidental delineations of the view.

## 1.

One Having the Name Shākya [Shākya Chok-den]: All these views of the Consequence School and the Autonomy School are well founded[b] meanings of the thought of the middle wheel of doctrine and Nāgārjuna's Collections of Reasonings and are also the literal explicit teaching of the middle wheel of doctrine. [However] what is explicitly indicated in Nāgārjuna's Collections of Reasonings and

---

[a] Near the end of this text (p. 133), Tāranātha says, "Since [Shākya Chok-den and Döl-b̄o-b̄a] are similar in asserting that the basic element is beyond terms and conceptions and in asserting that it is the object of non-conceptual unmistaken pristine wisdom, they do not differ with respect to the final essential."

[b] *thad ldan.*

in the final wheel of doctrine are not in agreement.

The Omniscient Great Jo-nang-b̄a [Döl-b̄o-b̄a S̄hay-rap-gyel-tsen]: Although the views of the Consequence School and the Autonomy School are claimed to be the thought of the middle wheel of doctrine and Nāgārjuna's Collections of Reasonings, they are not their unblemished thought. Although they seem to connect with what is explicitly indicated in the bulk of passages in the Collections of Reasonings, there are also many cases where they do not. Since many passages in the middle wheel of doctrine clearly teach other-emptiness, what is explicitly indicated in the middle wheel of doctrine and Nāgārjuna's Collections of Reasonings is not literal [that is, is not to be taken literally].

Concerning this, although what is explicitly indicated by the bulk of the passages in the middle wheel of doctrine and Nāgārjuna's Collections of Reasonings does not contradict either the Consequence and the Autonomy schools or other-emptiness, those that are cited as sources for the uncommon tenets of what is reputed to be self-emptiness serve as bases for making mistakes about those, but they do not teach those respective tenets. Since [the middle wheel of doctrine and Nāgārjuna's Collections of Reasonings] even have many uncommon passages—other than those—that contradict the systems of those [schools], and teach only other-emptiness, even the middle wheel of doctrine and Nāgārjuna's Collections of Reasonings teach other-emptiness itself.

Nevertheless, the uncommon [tenets of] other-emptiness *clearly and extensively* occur only in the final wheel of doctrine and the commentaries on their thought, and those [that is, the middle wheel of doctrine and Nāgārjuna's Collections of Reasonings] do not teach the uncommon tenets of the Consequence School and the Autonomy School that are reputed nowadays to be the view of self-emptiness. Rather, they extensively teach the self-emptiness that is the thought of the Conqueror [Buddha] as well as his children.

## 2.

Shākya Chok-den:[a] That Maitreya's *Ornament for Clear Realization* teaches both the tenets of self-emptiness and the tenets of other-emptiness is in consideration that:

- the self-emptiness [found] in the three—the Consequence School, the Autonomy School, and the model texts [of Nāgārjuna and Āryadeva]—is needed for eliminating proliferations through the view, and
- other-emptiness is needed for practice through meditation.

The four remaining Doctrines of Maitreya[b] indeed teach only other-emptiness, but among them there are two types: Maitreya's *Sublime Continuum of the Great Vehicle* sets forth one final vehicle and refutes that there are those whose [spiritual] lineage is severed, whereas the other three texts describe three final vehicles and severance of [spiritual] lineage.

Döl-b̄o-b̄a: The Five Doctrines of Maitreya do not at all have separate tenet systems. The tenets reputed to be self-emptiness are not set forth in Maitreya's *Ornament for Clear Realization,* and also Maitreya's *Ornament for the Great Vehicle Sūtras* and so forth do not set forth an utter severance of [spiritual] lineage and do not set forth three final vehicles.

## 3.

Shākya Chok-den: Self-emptiness is more profound for eliminating proliferations by means of the view. Other-emptiness is more profound for practice by means of meditation.

Döl-b̄o-b̄a: The view of self-emptiness that is asserted by the

---

[a] From here on, Tāranātha uses "the former" for Shākya Chok-den and "the latter" for Döl-b̄o-b̄a S̄hay-rap-gyel-tsen, explaining near the end of the text that the terms indicate not temporal order but a way of initiating discussion of a topic and responding to it with the favored opinion.

[b] These are the *Sublime Continuum of the Great Vehicle,* the *Differentiation of Phenomena and the Noumenon,* the *Differentiation of the Middle and the Extremes,* and the *Ornament for the Great Vehicle Sūtras.*

Conqueror as well as his children is the supreme eliminator of proliferations, but since it is included in other-emptiness, view and practice are not separate. Self-emptiness—the view of the Consequence School, Autonomy School, and the model texts [of Nāgārjuna and Āryadeva]—as it is nowadays reputed in which it is asserted that ultimate truth is without true existence—is a mistake. Hence, it is not appropriate to be a view eliminating proliferations since it is a deprecation.[a]

## 4.

Shākya Chok-den: Since other-emptiness surpasses Mind-Only, it suffices as Middle Way, but in terms of view self-emptiness is even higher than that. However, other-emptiness does not [thereby] come to be mistaken, since it accords with the meaning [realized] in meditation.[b]

Döl-b̄o-b̄a: Since even self-emptiness surpasses Mind-Only, self-emptiness is merely included in the Middle Way from among the four schools of tenets, but self-emptiness is not the pure final [Middle Way]. The highest of views is only other-emptiness.

## 5.

Shākya Chok-den: As the reason for that, in the Doctrines of Maitreya as well as their followers, analysis is not performed with respect to non-dual pristine wisdom, but since in general terms[c] even non-dual pristine wisdom does not withstand analysis when analyzed by reasoning, there is no possibility that anything withstands analysis by reasoning distinguishing the ultimate,[d] whereby the view

---

[a] Döl-b̄o-b̄a's *Mountain Doctrine* (24, 199, 205) depicts the middle wheel of doctrine as declaring that all phenomena, including the ultimate, are self-empty and that this view is effective for quieting conceptuality. Hence, Tāranātha's presentation appears to be a refinement of Döl-b̄o-b̄a's opinion.

[b] *sgom don dang mthun pa.*

[c] *spyi ldog nas.*

[d] *don dam gcod byed kyi rig pas.*

of self-emptiness is more profound. Though non-dual pristine wisdom does not withstand analysis, the continuum of experiencing that pristine wisdom is unbroken, due to which the meaning [realized] in meditation abides in accordance with other-emptiness.

Döl-b̄o-b̄a: Since non-dual pristine wisdom withstands analysis by reasoning, analysis of it [that seemingly shows that it cannot withstand analysis] is your own mistake.

## 6.

Shākya Chok-den: Non-dual pristine wisdom is a momentary knowing;[a] it not permanent; there is no opportunity for it to remain [for a second instant. Nevertheless, its continuum is unbroken.]

Döl-b̄o-b̄a: Non-dual pristine wisdom is not momentary. Since it is released from the three times, it is permanent and steady.[b]

## 7.

Shākya Chok-den: Because non-dual pristine wisdom is cognition,[c] it is an effective thing.[d]

Döl-b̄o-b̄a: Non-dual pristine wisdom is released from both effective things and non-things.

## 8.

Shākya Chok-den: Non-dual pristine wisdom is compounded.

Döl-b̄o-b̄a: [Self-arisen] non-dual pristine wisdom is uncompounded.

---

a *rig pa.*

b *rtag pa brtan pa.*

c *shes pa.*

d *dngos po.*

# 9.

Shākya Chok-den: In harmony with Tibetan [scholars] in general, the following is asserted. Just this luminous knowing that is the self-isolate[a] of all cognitions is the other-powered entity.[b] The imputational nature is from the viewpoint of the self-isolate of only the dualistic appearance that dawns to that [other-powered entity]; the other-powered nature is from the viewpoint of that luminous knowing together with that dualistic appearance; and the thoroughly established nature is from the viewpoint of the primordial non-pollution of dualistic phenomena in that luminous knowing. Hence, the other-powered nature and the thoroughly established nature are different from the viewpoint of their isolate factors and from the viewpoint of their defining characters, but the other-powered entity itself and the thoroughly established nature are the same entity.

Döl-b̄o-b̄a: Imputational factors imputed by various conceptual awarenesses and appearance factors that are appearances as external objects—that is to say, the self-isolate of apprehended factors[c]—are imputational natures. The self-isolate of cognition[d] in minds and mental factors—that is, conventional cognitions[e] or cognitions included within consciousness[f]—are other-powered natures. Naturally luminous knowing[g] devoid of proliferations is the thoroughly established nature. Therefore, although imputational natures do not exist as different substantial entities from other-powered natures, they are very different from the viewpoint of their defining characters. Thoroughly established natures and other-powered natures not only are different in their isolate factors and defining

---

a *rang ldog;* here the term means "the thing itself" or perhaps "essential nature."

b *gzhan dbang gi dngos po.*

c *gzung ba'i rang ldog.*

d *shes pa'i rang ldog.*

e *kun rdzob pa'i shes pa.*

f *rnam shes kyis bsdus pa'i shes pa.* Self-arisen pristine wisdom is cognition not included within consciousness.

g *rang bzhin gsal rig.*

characters, they are also not the same entity. The former presentation [by Shākya Chok-den and other Tibetan scholars] is largely in harmony with Mind-Only, whereas the Middle Way is only this. That is [my, that is, Döl-b̄o-b̄a's] thought.

# 10.

For those reasons[a] Shākya Chok-den says: Imputational natures are necessarily without true existence. Thoroughly established natures necessarily truly exist. Other-powered natures have both types.

Döl-b̄o-b̄a: Both imputational natures and other-powered natures necessarily are one-pointedly without true existence.

# 11.

Likewise, Shākya Chok-den says: All self-cognitions[b] are only ultimates in terms of the self-isolate of self-cognition.[c]

Döl-b̄o-b̄a: Self-cognitions of conventional consciousnesses are only conventional. Hence, there are two—conventional and ultimate self-cognitions.

# 12.

Shākya Chok-den: Thoroughly established natures are emptinesses. Although imputational natures are just empty, they are not emptinesses. Emptinesses are necessarily ultimates.

Döl-b̄o-b̄a: All phenomena and noumena must be said to be just emptinesses. Emptinesses are not necessarily ultimates. Do not apply modes of entailment with regard to the synonyms [of emptiness; the above two statements] are to be applied to the main meaning.[d]

---

[a] That is to say, Shākya Chok-den's exposition in the ninth point.

[b] *rang rig.*

[c] *rang rig gi rang ldog nas;* this is self-cognition in isolation, just the essence of self-cognition.

[d] Perhaps this means that although the term "noumenon," for instance,

# 13.

Likewise, Shākya Chok-den says, largely in harmony with the general vocabulary of the texts of valid cognition, manifest knowledge, and so forth:

- Whatever is an established base[a] (*gzhi grub*) is necessarily either an effective thing (*dngos po*) or a non-thing (*dngos med*).
- Whatever is a consciousness (*shes pa*) is necessarily an effective thing.
- The ultimate is an effective thing.[b]
- The uncompounded are the non-things space and so forth.
- Thusness (*de bzhin nyid*) is not compounded by karma and afflictive emotions, and sheer luminous knowing (*gsal rig tsam*) is not *newly* compounded. Since these and others each have uncompounded factors, they are imputed to be uncompounded by way of verbal variants (*rnam grangs kyi sgo nas*), but they are not the uncompounded in the sense of having a character contradictory with compositional phenomena (*'du byed*). Hence, they are imputed uncompoundeds (*'dus ma byas btags pa ba*) [but not actual uncompoundeds].

Döl-b̄o-b̄a: Those explanations in [the texts of] valid cognition, manifest knowledge, and so forth are a system mainly delineating conventionalities. On this occasion of the definitive meaning in

---

is a synonym of "emptiness," it solely refers to other-emptiness and thus is solely ultimate, whereas "emptiness" refers to both self-emptiness (which is conventional) and other-emptiness (which is ultimate).

[a] That is to say, an existent (*yod pa*).

[b] Both texts (Dzamthang edition, 215.2, and Leh edition, 787.4) read *don dam dngos po **min*** ("The ultimate **is not** an effective thing."); however, given Shākya Chok-den's opinions expressed in items seven ("Because non-dual pristine wisdom is cognition, it is an effective thing.") and eight ("Non-dual pristine wisdom is compounded.") as well as the material following the present passage, it appears that this line should read *don dam dngos po **yin*** ("The ultimate **is** an effective thing.") The Leh edition, which is photo-offset, exhibits signs of untutored altering of the photo, most likely changing *yin* to *min*.

which the ultimate is mainly being delineated:

- Whatever is a conventionality is necessarily an effective thing or a non-thing, and also whatever is an effective thing or a non-thing is necessarily a conventionality.
- Since the ultimate is neither an effective thing nor a non-thing, whatever is an established base is not necessarily an effective thing or a non-thing.
- Since pristine wisdom is not an effective thing but is a cognition (*shes pa*), whatever is a cognition is not necessarily an effective thing.
- The assertion that a non-thing is an ultimate is very unreasonable, and the assertion that an ultimate is an effective thing is the system of Proponents of Effective Things (*dngos smra ba*).
- Since on this occasion even all non-things such as space and so forth—which the Proponents of Manifest Knowledge (*mngon pa ba rnams*) assert as uncompounded—are [actually] compounded, whatever is an effective thing or a non-thing is necessarily compounded.
- The ultimate is the actual uncompounded (*'dus ma byas dngos*); space and so forth are imputed uncompoundeds.

## 14.

Also, Shākya Chok-den says: The self-natures of other-powered natures[a] are the bases of emptiness, and their emptiness of the imputational nature that is the object of negation[b] is itself the ultimate empty of conventionalities (*kun rdzob kyis stong pa'i don dam*).

Döl-b̄o-b̄a: The bases of emptiness, thoroughly established natures, are empty of the two objects of negation, other-powered natures and imputational natures. This is the meaning of the ultimate empty of conventionalities. Other-powered natures' emptiness of imputational natures is asserted only on an occasion of delineating just obscurational truths.

---

a *gzhan dbang gi rang ngo.*

b *dgag bya kun btags kyis stong pa.*

## 15.

Shākya Chok-den: Although "pure other-powered natures" (*dag pa gzhan dbang*) are renowned in general Tibet, in fact they are not other-powered natures, but are undistorted thoroughly established natures (*phyin ci ma log pa'i yongs grub*). Furthermore, undistorted thoroughly established natures are actual thoroughly established natures. Since even the convention "pure other-powered natures" has no clear source, the usage of this terminology is not considered to be good.

Döl-b̄o-b̄a: Although the convention "pure other-powered natures" does not clearly appear in the [source] texts, the meaning is contained there, due to which it is suitable to use the convention. This is because the Buddha's teaching is to rely on the meaning, and since all earlier Tibetans in harmony used the convention "pure other-powered natures," it is fit to be an unmistaken quintessential instruction transmitted from Maitreya. Although among that [category of pure other-powered natures] certain pristine wisdoms of learner Superiors [such as other-arisen pristine wisdoms] are undistorted thoroughly established natures, those who have attained a [Bodhisattva] ground also have certain [pure other-powered natures]—such as perceiving the ground to be gold and so forth—that are undistorted thoroughly established natures. Hence, the presentation of that convention is considered to be good.

## 16.

Shākya Chok-den: It is asserted that whatever is a undistorted thoroughly established nature is necessarily a fully qualified thoroughly established nature.

Döl-b̄o-b̄a: Those are merely indicated to be *enumerated* thoroughly established natures,[a] like calling even the twelve branches of scripture "thoroughly established natures." Therefore, the undistorted that are adduced in a pair with immutable thoroughly established natures are pure other-powered natures and imputed thor-

---

[a] *rnam grangs kyi yongs grub.*

oughly established natures. The undistorted thoroughly established natures that are the same as the immutable [thoroughly established natures] are called "ultimate undistorted thoroughly established natures"; they are only immutable [thoroughly established natures]. Hence, on occasions of delineating the mode of subsistence the thoroughly established nature is suchness, whereas on occasions of extensive descriptions of enumerations a twofold presentation is made.

## 17.

Shākya Chok-den: Even [certain] true paths are taken to be ultimate truths.

Döl-b̄o-b̄a: True cessations in the division into four truths are asserted to be ultimates, and the other three truths are asserted to be conventionalities. In detail, fully qualified true cessations—that is to say, primordial true cessations—are necessarily only ultimate truths, and the other three truths and individual analytic cessations are necessarily conventionalities. Since this is the case,

- fully qualified true paths are necessarily conventionalities
- fully qualified true cessations are necessarily ultimate truths
- ultimate true paths are the same as the primordial, due to which they are just true cessations and hence imputed true paths.

## 18.

Shākya Chok-den: The matrix-of-One-Gone-to-Bliss does not exist in the continuums of sentient beings.[a] The clear light nature of the mind of a sentient being is the mere cause of and constituent of the matrix-of-One-Gone-to-Bliss.[b] Therefore, although a causal matrix-

---

[a] For Shākya Chok-den, in the context of three levels of persons (impure, impure-pure, and pure) in Maitreya's *Sublime Continuum* the term "sentient beings" excludes not only Buddhas but also Bodhisattvas from the first ground up. Thanks to Yaroslav Komarovski for the distinction.

[b] *bde gzhegs snying po'i rgyu dang khams tsam.*

of-One-Gone-to-Bliss[a] or constitutive matrix-of-One-Gone-to-Bliss[b] exists in all sentient beings, it is not fully qualified. Just the pristine wisdom of a Buddha is the matrix-of-One-Gone-to-Bliss.

Döl-b̄o-b̄a: This one itself in the continuum of a sentient being is a fully qualified matrix-of-One-Gone-to-Bliss. If a Buddha is fully qualified, then since it itself is the noumenon of sentient beings, sentient beings are established as possessing the matrix-of-One-Gone-to-Bliss, and in particular, this is established by endless scriptures. Descriptions of it as constituent and cause are in consideration of basic element[c] and separative cause,[d] not in consideration of producing constituent[e] and producing cause.[f]

## 19.

Shākya Chok-den: That the matrix is said to be naturally endowed with [Buddha-]qualities as an inseparable entity is [in reference] only to the state of the fruit [of Buddhahood]. On the occasion of the cause [that is, the basal state], there are mere seeds that are capacities suitable for the arising of qualities.

Döl-b̄o-b̄a: Qualities that are an inseparable entity and naturally endowed exist also in the basal matrix-of-One-Gone-to-Bliss because the newly arisen could not be among the naturally endowed and because the three—basis, path, and fruit [matrixes-of-One-Gone-to-Bliss]—except for being differentiated by way of conventional substrata are only the sole natural matrix-of-One-Gone-to-Bliss. Once it is a matrix-of-One-Gone-to-Bliss, it must be adorned with all ultimate qualities.

---

a *rgyu bde gzhegs snying po.*

b *khams bde gzhegs snying po.*

c *dbyings.*

d *bral rgyu.*

e *skyed khams.*

f *skyed rgyu.*

# 20.

Shākya Chok-den: Marks, beauties, and so forth are not asserted with respect to the qualities of the body of attributes.

Döl-b̄o-b̄a: With respect to all types of Buddha-qualities there are ultimate qualities of the body of attributes that are appearances to Buddhas themselves[a] and conventional qualities of form bodies that are appearances to others, trainees.[b] The *Sūtra Requested by the Precious Girl*[c] and the explicit teaching of Maitreya's *Sublime Continuum of the Great Vehicle* give mere exemplifications [of certain qualities as factors of the body of attributes and some qualities as factors of form bodies][d] in accordance with general renown in terms of predominance, this being within [the context that] in general the qualities of both bodies must be complete. In accordance with other sūtras, the tantra sets, and so forth both [the body of attributes and the form bodies] have factors of all [qualities].

# 21.

Now on the occasion of Mantra the difference with respect to other-emptiness is as follows.
Shākya Chok-den: Mere seeds of the fruit exist integrally in the

---

[a] *sangs rgyas rang snang.*

[b] *gdul bya gzhan snang.*

[c] *bu mo rin chen gyis zhus pa'i mdo, ratnadārikāsūtra.*

[d] As, for instance, when Maitreya's *Sublime Continuum of the Great Vehicle* (III.3) says:

> The first, the body [of attributes], is [indivisibly] endowed with
> The separative qualities [—discerned by merely separating from obstructions through accumulating the collections of pristine wisdom—the ten] powers, [four fearlessnesses,] and so forth.
> The second, [form bodies,] possess the qualities
> Of the [thirty-two] marks [and so forth] of a great being that are [gradual] maturations [from having accumulated collections of merit].

This is cited in Döl-b̄o-b̄a's *Mountain Doctrine,* 426; brackets are from Döl-b̄o-b̄a's *Rays of the Sun,* 151.6.

clear light nature of the mind. Through meditative cultivation of the path, enhancement is attained. Finally the fruit arises in manifestation.

Döl-b̄o-b̄a: Pristine wisdom that is spontaneously primordially complete in the ultimate maṇḍala is manifested upon removing defilements through meditatively cultivating the path.

In laying out those different assertions in that way, [I] have used "the former"[a] with the sense of starting the discussion and "latter" with the sense of supporting the tradition.[b] Since that was the intention, these should also be associated with the remaining assertions in accordance with how they were stated on the occasion of the first assertion [when the protagonists were identified as "One Having the Name Shākya" and "The Omniscient Great Jo-nang-b̄a". The terms "former" and "latter"] do not indicate the order of the historical appearance of the composers of those tenet systems.

Concerning those, the reasons for the arising of that many different incidental[c] assertions mostly stem from a single root. What is that single root? The great paṇḍita named Shākya asserts that non-dual pristine wisdom has a nature not of being one[d] but of being manifold,[e] and is impermanent, not abiding for an instant.[f] The omniscient Jo-nang-b̄a [Döl-b̄o-b̄a S̄hay-rap-gyel-tsen] asserts that although in actual fact[g] non-dual pristine wisdom is indeed definite

---

[a] *snga ma;* except for the first of the twenty-one Tāranātha uses "the former" to indicate Shākya Chok-den, and "the latter" (*phyi ma*) to indicate Döl-b̄o-b̄a, which I have translated with their respective names. His point here is that "former" and "latter" do not indicate historical order.

[b] *gzhung 'dzugs.*

[c] *gnas skabs;* as opposed to the fundamental issue, on which those who perceive the profound agree, as Tāranātha says in the expression of worship at the beginning of the text.

[d] *gcig.*

[e] *du ma.*

[f] For Shākya Chok-den non-dual pristine wisdom is momentary, not abiding for a second moment.

[g] *dngos gnas la.* In *Mountain Doctrine* (31ff.), Döl-b̄o-b̄a makes a dis-

as not one or manifold, provisionally a presentation of it as one is correct, and it is permanent due to asserting it as being partless, all-pervasive, devoid of proliferation, and devoid of predication. In brief, they differ in asserting it to be impermanent and permanent.

Since [Shākya Chok-den and Döl-b̄o-b̄a] are similar in asserting that the basic element[a] is beyond terms and conceptions and in asserting that it is the object of non-conceptual unmistaken pristine wisdom, they do not differ with respect to the final essential. Therefore, the glorious great Jo-nang-b̄a, knowing such, understood through rational analysis that:

- Because of being partless and because of being all-pervasive the noumenon is only one in the individual environments and beings therein, in the threefold basis, path, and fruit, and in all Buddhas and sentient beings.
- And for that reason the matrix-of-One-Gone-to-Bliss is endowed with all [ultimate Buddha-]qualities.
- And for that reason [the noumenon] is not damaged by the reasoning of dependent-arising, the lack of being one or many, and so forth, and hence withstands analysis.
- And since that is the case, the uncommon tenets of the Autonomists and Consequentialists, who assert that [the noumenon] falls apart under analysis, are in error, and hence the views of the Autonomy School and the Consequence School are incorrect[b] and therefore do not accord with the thought of the middle wheel of doctrine.
- and so forth.

With respect to the teaching in Maitreya's *Ornament for the Great Vehicle Sūtras* that there is one [final] vehicle and the assertion that an utter severance of [spiritual] lineage is to be refuted, the sole

tinction between occasions of conclusive setting in profound meditative equipoise free from all proliferations and occasions of making distinctions, whereas Tāranātha calls the former "in actual fact" and the latter "provisionally" or "for the time being" (*gnas skabs su*).

[a] *dbyings, dhātu.*

[b] *ma dag pa.*

feature described above does not stem[a] from them; rather, the others are by way of the former essential.[b]

Through taking hold of such definitive final tenets, one takes hold of the treasury of the secret mind of all Buddhas. When this ultimate lion's roar was proclaimed by the Great Omniscient Jo-nang-b̄a, all contemporaneous bearers of the discipline of the fortunate lion[c] gained enthusiasm, but later all the foxes of low lot were frightened as in the statement:

> Why is the profound not an object of logic?
> Why are those knowing the profound meaning liberated?

Later, from hearing these tenets, the hearts of the three—S̄a-ḡya-b̄as, Ge-luk-b̄as, and Ḡa-gyu-b̄as—as well as some N̄ying-ma-b̄as split open, and their brains were confounded, due to which, crazed by wrong conceptions, they were beclouded. Thereby reduced to babbling, they spewed forth awful explanations comprising deprecations and quasi-reasoning. Nevertheless, it appears that even at this end of an era some having good fortune regarding the profound meaning have attained triply aspected belief in the style of "If scholars analyze it properly, they will not be frightened by this doctrine."

Furthermore, real permanence[d] is not a permanent non-thing, which is the mere opposite of impermanence.[e] It is also not the compounded permanence that is a permanence of continuum.[f] It is also not a permanent effective thing,[g] asserted by [non-Buddhist] Forders, that does not occur among objects of knowledge. It is also not a negative permanence that is a mere meaning-generality.[h] It is

---

a *bsten pa.*

b All these points derive from the assertion that self-arisen pristine wisdom is permanent.

c *gdong lnga;* literally "five-tufted."

d *yang dag pa'i rtag pa.*

e *mi rtag pa log tsam gyi rtag pa dngos med.*

f *rgyun gyi rtag pa.*

g *rtag dngos.*

h *dgag pa'i rtag pa don spyi tsam.*

also not asserted as the likes of a positive self-powered permanence.[a] [Rather] it is devoid of proliferations, the immutable basic element released from the proliferations of impermanent positive effective things[b] and negative permanent non-things.[c] Though it is released from the signs of permanence and released from the proliferations of permanence, it is immutable,[d] and hence is solely-permanent.[e]

*Question:* Well then, why does [non-dual pristine wisdom] also not become an impermanence that is released from the signs and proliferations of impermanence?[f]

*Answer:* That would be true if that nature had a factor of steady mutability,[g] but since such does not exist, a presentation positing it as impermanent is not made. Hence, being devoid of the proliferations of permanence and impermanence, it is indeed not a proliferative permanence[h] and is also not a proliferative impermanence; however, since an impermanence devoid of proliferations does not occur, it is not such, but is a permanence devoid of proliferations. That statement is the meaning of the thought of the profound matrix sūtras, the most secret from among the thoughts of all Conquerors.[i]

If good intelligence, merit, and
Supremely powerful blessings come together,
Belief will be attained in this,
But not through merely claiming to be wise.

---

a *sgrub pa rang dbang can gyi rtag pa.*

b *dngos po sgrub pa mi rtag pa.*

c *dngos med dgag pa rtag pa.*

d *mi 'gyur ba.*

e *rtag pa kho na.*

f *mi rtag pa'i mtshan ma dang spros pa las grol ba'i mi rtag pa.*

g The Smanrtsis Shesrig Dpemzod edition reads *rang bzhin de **la** 'gyur ba brtan pa'i cha yod na* ("if that nature had a factor of steady mutability"), whereas the Dzamthang edition reads *rang bzhin de **las** 'gyur ba brtan pa'i cha yod na* ("if it had a factor of steady mutability from that nature").

h *spros pa'i rtag pa.*

i *snying po'i mdo zab mo rnams kyi dgongs don rgyal ba thams cad kyi dgongs pa las ches gsang ba'o.*

This called *Twenty-one Differences Regarding the Profound Meaning* has been uttered by Tāranātha for the sake of those of low intelligence.

Corrected once.

Maṅgalaṃ

# List of Abbreviations

"Dharma" refers to the *sde dge* edition of the Tibetan canon published by Dharma Press: the *Nying-ma Edition of the sDe-dge bKa'-'gyur and bsTan-'gyur* (Oakland, Calif.: Dharma Press, 1980).

"Golden Reprint" refers to the *gser bris bstan 'gyur* (Sichuan, China: krung go'i mtho rim nang bstan slob gling gi bod brgyud nang bstan zhib 'jug khang, 1989).

"Karmapa *sde dge*" refers to the *sde dge mtshal par bka' 'gyur: A Facsimile Edition of the 18th Century Redaction of Si tu chos kyi 'byung gnas Prepared under the Direction of H.H. the 16th rgyal dbang karma pa* (Delhi: Delhi Karmapae Chodhey Gyalwae Sungrab Partun Khang, 1977).

"P," standing for "Peking edition," refers to the *Tibetan Tripitaka* (Tokyo-Kyoto: Tibetan Tripitaka Research Foundation, 1955-1962).

"*stog* Palace" refers to the *Tog Palace Manuscript of the Tibetan Kanjur* (Leh, Ladakh: Smanrtsis Shesrig Dpemdzod, 1979).

"Toh." refers to *A Complete Catalogue of the Tibetan Buddhist Canons,* edited by Hakuju Ui et al. (Sendai, Japan: Tohoku University, 1934), and *A Catalogue of the Tohoku University Collection of Tibetan Works on Buddhism,* edited by Yensho Kanakura et al. (Sendai, Japan: Tohoku University, 1953).

"Tokyo *sde dge*" refers to the *sDe dge Tibetan Tripiṭaka—bsTan ḥgyur preserved at the Faculty of Letters, University of Tokyo,* edited by Z. Yamaguchi et al. (Tokyo: Tokyo University Press, 1977-1984).

# Bibliography

Sūtras and tantras are listed alphabetically by English title in the first section of the Bibliography. Indian and Tibetan treatises are listed alphabetically by author in the second section, together with their translations.

## 1. Sūtras and Tantras


*Aṅgulimāla Sūtra*
aṅgulimālīyasūtra
sor mo'i phreng ba la phan pa'i mdo
P879, vol. 34
English translation of chap. 1: Nathan S. Cutler. "The Sutra of Sor-mo'i Phreng-ba (from the Lhasa, Peking, and Derge editions of the bKa'-'gyur)." Master's thesis, Indiana University, 1981.

*Buddhāvataṃsaka Sūtra*
buddhāvataṃsakanāma-mahāvaipulyasūtra
sangs rgyas phal po che zhes bya ba shin tu rgyas pa chen po'i mdo
P761, vols. 25-26

*Cloud of Jewels Sūtra*
ratnameghasūtra
dkon mchog spring gyi mdo
P879, vol. 35; Toh. 231, vol. wa

*Descent into Laṅkā Sūtra*
laṅkāvatārasūtra
lang kar gshegs pa'i mdo
P775, vol. 29
Sanskrit: Bunyiu Nanjio. *Bibl. Otaniensis,* vol. 1. Kyoto: Otani University Press, 1923. Also: P. L. Vaidya. *Saddharmalaṅkāvatārasūtram.* Buddhist Sanskrit Texts 3. Darbhanga, India: Mithila Institute, 1963.
English translation: D. T. Suzuki. *The Lankavatara Sutra.* London: Routledge and Kegan Paul, 1932.

*Eight Thousand Stanza Perfection of Wisdom Sūtra*
aṣṭasāhasrikāprajñāpāramitā
shes rab kyi pha rol tu phyin pa brgyad stong pa
P734, vol. 21
Sanskrit: P. L. Vaidya. *Aṣṭasāhasrika Prajñāpāramitā, with Haribhadra's Commentary called Ālokā.* Buddhist Sanskrit Texts 4. Darbhanga, India: Mithila Institute, 1960.
English translation: Edward Conze. *The Perfection of Wisdom in Eight Thousand Lines & Its Verse Summary.* Bolinas, Calif.: Four Seasons Foundation, 1973.

*Excellent Golden Light Sūtra*
suvarṇaprabhāsottamasūtrendrarāja
gser 'od dam pa mdo sde'i dbang po'i rgyal po
P174, 175, and 176, vols. 6-7
Tibetan and Chinese texts: Johannes Nobel. *Suvarṇaprabhāsottamasūtra. Das Goldglanz-Sūtra; ein Sanskrittext des Mahāyāna-Buddhismus.* Leiden: E.J. Brill, 1958.

Sanskrit: Johannes Nobel, ed. *Suvarnaprabhāsottamasūtra: Das Goldglanz-Sūtra; ein Sanskrittext des Mahāyāna-Buddhismus.* Leipzig: O. Harrassowitz, 1937.

*Expression of Mañjushrī's Ultimate Names Tantra*
mañjuśrījñānasattvasyaparamārthanāmasaṃgīti
'jam dpal ye shes sems dpa'i don dam pa'i mtshan yang dar par brjod pa
P2, vol. 1
English translation and Sanskrit edition: Ronald M. Davidson. "The Litany of Names of Mañjuśrī." In *Tantric and Taoist Studies in Honour of R.A. Stein,* edited by Michel Strickmann, vol. 1, 1-69. Mélanges Chinois et Bouddhiques, vol. 20. Brussels: Institut Belge des Hautes Études Chinoises, 1981. Translation reprinted, with minor changes, in: Ronald M. Davidson. "The Litany of Names of Mañjuśrī." In *Religions of India in Practice,* edited by Donald S. Lopez, Jr., 104-125. Princeton, N.J.: Princeton University Press, 1995.

*Five Hundred Stanza Perfection of Wisdom Sūtra*
āryapañcaśatikāprajñāpāramitā
'phags pa shes rab kyi pha rol tu phyin pa lnga brgya pa
P0738, vol. 21.
English translation: Edward Conze. *The Short Prajñāpāramitā Texts.* London: Luzac, 1973.

*Great Drum Sūtra*
mahābherīhārakaparivartasūtra
rnga bo che chen po'i le'u'i mdo
P888, vol. 35

*Magical Meditative Stabilization Ascertaining Peace Sūtra*
praśāntaviniścayaprātihāryanāmasamādhisūtra
rab tu zhi ba rnam par nges pa'i cho 'phrul gyi ting nge 'dzin gyi mdo
P797, vol. 32

*Mahāparinirvāṇa Sūtra*
āryamahāparinirvāṇanāmamahāyānasūtra
'phags pa yongs su mya ngan las 'das pa chen po'i mdo
P787, vols. 30-31; translated by Wang phab shun, dGe ba'i blo gros, and rGya mtsho'i sde in fourteen chapters
P788, vol. 31; translated by Jinamitra, Jñānagarbha, and Lha'i zla ba in four chapters
English translation from the Chinese: Kosho Yamamoto. *The Mahāyāna Mahāparinirvāṇa-sutra.* Ube, Japan: Karinbunko, 1973.

*Matrix-of-One-Gone-Thus Sūtra*
āryatathāgatagarbhanāmamahāyanasūtra
'phags pa de bzhin gshegs pa'i snying po zhes bya ba theg pa chen po'i mdo
P924, vol. 36
English translation: William H. Grosnick. "The *Tathāgatagarbha Sūtra.*" In *Buddhism in Practice,* edited by Donald S. Lopez, Jr., 92-106. Princeton: Princeton University Press, 1995. Also: Shu-hui J. Chen. "Affirmation in Negation: A Study of the Tathāgatagarbha Theory in the Light of the Bodhisattva Practices," 457-503. Ph.D. diss., University of Wisconsin-Madison, 1998.

*Perfection of Wisdom Sūtra in One Hundred Thousand Stanzas*
śatasāhasrikāprajñāpāramitā
shes rab kyi pha rol tu phyin pa stong phrag brgya pa
P730, vols.12-18; Toh. 8, vols. ka-a (*'bum*)

Condensed English translation: Edward Conze. *The Large Sūtra on Perfect Wisdom.* Berkeley: University of California Press, 1975.

*Pile of Jewels Sūtra*

ratnakūṭa / mahāratnakūṭadharmaparyāyaśatasāhasrikagrantha

dkon brtsegs / dkon mchog brtsegs pa chen po'i chos kyi rnam grangs le'u stong phrag brgya pa

P760, vols. 22-24

*Questions of King Dhāraṇīshvara Sūtra / Sūtra Teaching the Great Compassion of a One Gone Thus*

āryatathāgatamahākaruṇānirdeśasūtra

de bzhin gshegs pa'i snying rje chen po bstan pa'i mdo / 'phags pa gzungs kyi dbang phyug rgyal pos zhus pa'i mdo

P814, vol. 32

*Shrīmālādevī Sūtra*

āryaśrīmālādevīsiṃhanādanāmamahāyanasūtra

phags pa lha mo dpal phreng gi seng ge'i sgra zhes bya ba theg pa chen po'i mdo

P760.48, vol. 24

English translation: Alex Wayman and Hideko Wayman. *The Lion's Roar of Queen Śrīmālā: A Buddhist Scripture on the Tathāgatagarbha Theory.* New York: Columbia University Press, 1974.

*Sūtra on the Heavily Adorned Array*

ghanavyūhasūtra

rgyan stug po bkod pa'i mdo

P778, vol. 29

*Sūtra Requested by the Precious Girl*

ratnadārikāsūtra

bu mo rin chen gyis zhus pa'i mdo

P (?)

*Sūtra Unraveling the Thought*

saṃdhinirmocanasūtra

dgongs pa nges par 'grel pa'i mdo

P774, vol. 29; Toh 106; Dharma, vol. 18; *stog* Palace, vol. 63, 1-160 (Leh: Smanrtsis Shesrig Dpemzod, 1975-1978)

Tibetan text and French translation: Étienne Lamotte. *Saṃdhinirmocanasūtra: L'explication des mystères.* Louvain: Université de Louvain, 1935.

English translation: C. John Powers. *Wisdom of Buddha: Saṁdhinirmocana Sūtra.* Berkeley: Dharma Publishing, 1995. Also: Thomas Cleary. *Buddhist Yoga: A Comprehensive Course.* Boston: Shambhala, 1995.

## 2. Other Sanskrit and Tibetan Works

Anubhūtisvarūpācārya

*Sārasvatī's Grammar Sūtra*

sārasvatavyākaraṇa / sārasvatīprakriyā

brda sprod dbyangs can/ dbyangs can sgra mdo/ dbyangs can ma

P5886, vol. 148; P5911, vol. 149; P5912, vol. 149

Asaṅga (*thogs med,* fourth century)

*Explanation of (Maitreya's) "Sublime Continuum of the Great Vehicle"*

mahāynottaratantraśāstravyākhya

theg pa chen po'i rgyud bla ma'i bstan bcos kyi rnam par bshad pa
P5526, vol. 108
Sanskrit: E. H. Johnston (and T. Chowdhury). *The Ratnagotravibhāga Mahāyānottaratantraśāstra.* Patna, India: Bihar Research Society, 1950.
English translation: E. Obermiller. "Sublime Science of the Great Vehicle to Salvation." *Acta Orientalia* 9 (1931): 81-306. Also: J. Takasaki. *A Study on the Ratnagotravibhāga.* Serie Orientale Roma 33. Rome: Istituto Italiano per il Medio ed Estremo Oriente, 1966.

**Five Treatises on the Grounds**

1. *Grounds of Yogic Practice*
yogācārabhūmi
rnal 'byor spyod pa'i sa
P5536-5538, vols. 109-110
*Grounds of Bodhisattvas*
Bodhisattvabhūmi
byang chub sems pa'i sa
P5538, vol. 110
Sanskrit: Unrai Wogihara. *Bodhisattvabhūmi: A Statement of the Whole Course of the Bodhisattva (Being the Fifteenth Section of Yogācārabhūmi).* Leipzig: 1908; Tokyo: Seigo Kenyūkai, 1930-1936. Also: Nalinaksha Dutt. *Bodhisattvabhumi (Being the XVth Section of Asangapada's Yogacarabhumi).* Tibetan Sanskrit Works Series 7. Patna, India: K. P. Jayaswal Research Institute, 1966.
English translation of the Chapter on Suchness, the fourth chapter of Part I which is the fifteenth volume of the *Grounds of Yogic Practice:* Janice D. Willis. *On Knowing Reality.* New York: Columbia University Press, 1979; reprint, Delhi: Motilal Banarsidass, 1979.
2. *Compendium of Ascertainments*
nirṇayasaṃgraha / viniścayasaṃgrahaṇī
rnam par gtan la dbab pa bsdu ba
P5539, vols. 110-111
3. *Compendium of Bases*
vastusaṃgraha
gzhi bsdu ba
P5540, vol. 111
4. *Compendium of Enumerations*
paryāyasaṃgraha
rnam grang bsdu ba
P5543, vol. 111
5. *Compendium of Explanations*
vivaraṇasaṃgraha
rnam par bshad pa bsdu ba
P5543, vol. 111

*Grounds of Hearers*
nyan sa
śrāvakabhūmi
P5537, vol. 110
Sanskrit: Karunesha Shukla. *Śrāvakabhūmi.* Tibetan Sanskrit Works Series 14. Patna, India: K. P. Jayaswal Research Institute, 1973.

**Two Summaries**

1. *Summary of Manifest Knowledge*
   abhidharmasamuccaya
   chos mngon pa kun btus
   P5550, vol. 112
   Sanskrit: Pralhad Pradhan. *Abhidharma Samuccaya of Asaṅga.* Visva-Bharati Series 12. Santiniketan, India: Visva-Bharati (Santiniketan Press), 1950.
   French translation: Walpola Rahula. *La compendium de la super-doctrine (philosophie) (Abhidharmasamuccaya) d'Asaṅga.* Paris: École Française d'Extrême-Orient, 1971.
   English translation from the French: Walpola Rahula. *Abhidharmasamuccaya: The Compendium of the Higher Teaching (Philosophy) by Asaṅga.* Trans. Sara Boin-Webb. Fremont, Calif.: Asian Humanities Press, 2001.
2. *Summary of the Great Vehicle*
   mahāyānasaṃgraha
   theg pa chen po bsdus pa
   P5549, vol. 112
   French translation and Chinese and Tibetan texts: Étienne Lamotte. *La somme du grand véhicule d'Asaṅga.* 2 vols. Publications de l'Institute Orientaliste de Louvain 8. Louvain: Université de Louvain, 1938; reprint, 1973.
   English translation: John P. Keenan. *The Summary of the Great Vehicle by Bodhisattva Asaṅga: Translated from the Chinese of Paramārtha.* Berkeley, Calif.: Numata Center for Buddhist Translation and Research, 1992.

Bhāvaviveka (*legs ldan 'byed,* c. 500-570?)

*Blaze of Reasoning / Commentary on the "Heart of the Middle": Blaze of Reasoning*
madhyamakahṛdayavṛttitarkajvālā
dbu ma'i snying po'i 'grel pa rtog ge 'bar ba
P5256, vol. 96
Partial English translation (chap. 3, 1-136): Shōtarō Iida. *Reason and Emptiness.* Tokyo: Hokuseido, 1980.

Chandrakīrti (*candrakīrti, zla ba grags pa,* seventh century)

*[Auto]commentary on the "Supplement to (Nāgārjuna's) 'Treatise on the Middle'"*
madhaymakāvatārabhāṣya
dbu ma la 'jug pa'i bshad pa / dbu ma la 'jug pa'i rang 'grel
P5263, vol. 98. Also: Dharamsala, India: Council of Religious and Cultural Affairs, 1968.
Tibetan: Louis de La Vallée Poussin. *Madhyamakāvatāra par Candrakīrti.* Bibliotheca Buddhica 9. Osnabrück, Germany: Biblio Verlag, 1970.
English translation: C. W. Huntington, Jr. *The Emptiness of Emptiness: An Introduction to Early Indian Mādhyamika,* 147-195. Honolulu: University of Hawaii Press, 1989.
French translation (up to chap. 6, stanza 165): Louis de La Vallée Poussin. *Muséon* 8 (1907): 249-317; *Muséon* 11 (1910): 271-358; *Muséon* 12 (1911): 235-328.
German translation (chap. 6, stanzas 166-226): Helmut Tauscher. *Candrakīrti-Madhyamakāvatāraḥ und Madhyamakāvatārabhāṣyam.* Vienna: Arbeitskreis für Tibetische und Buddhistische Studien, Universität Wien, 1981.

*Clear Words, Commentary on (Nāgārjuna's) "Treatise on the Middle"*
mūlamadhyamakavṛttiprasannapadā
dbu ma rtsa ba'i 'grel pa tshig gsal ba
P5260, vol. 98. Also: Dharamsala, India: Tibetan Cultural Printing Press, 1968.
Sanskrit: Louis de La Vallée Poussin. *Mūlamadhyamakakārikās de Nāgārjuna avec la*

*Prasannapadā commentaire de Candrakīrti.* Bibliotheca Buddhica 4. Osnabrück, Germany: Biblio Verlag, 1970.

English translation (chap. 1, 25): T. Stcherbatsky. *Conception of Buddhist Nirvāṇa,* 77-222. Leningrad: Office of the Academy of Sciences of the USSR, 1927; rev. reprint, Delhi: Motilal Banarsidass, 1978.

English translation (chap. 2): Jeffrey Hopkins. "Analysis of Coming and Going." Dharamsala, India: Library of Tibetan Works and Archives, 1974.

Partial English translation: Mervyn Sprung. *Lucid Exposition of the Middle Way: The Essential Chapters from the Prasannapadā of Candrakīrti translated from the Sanskrit.* London: Routledge, 1979; Boulder, Colo.: Prajñā Press, 1979.

French translation (chapters 2-4, 6-9, 11, 23, 24, 26, 28): Jacques May. *Prasannapadā Madhyamaka-vṛtti, douze chapitres traduits du sanscrit et du tibétain.* Paris: Adrien-Maisonneuve, 1959.

French translation (chapters 18-22): J. W. de Jong. *Cinq chapitres de la Prasannapadā.* Paris: Geuthner, 1949.

German translation (chap. 5, 12-26): Stanislaw Schayer. *Ausgewählte Kapitel aus der Prasannapadā.* Krakow: Naktadem Polskiej Akademji Umiejetnosci, 1931.

German translation (chap. 10): Stanislaw Schayer. "Feuer und Brennstoff." *Rocznik Orjentalistyczny* 7 (1931):26-52.

D̄ak-tsang Ṡhay-rap-rin-chen (*stag tshang lo tsā ba shes rab rin chen,* b. 1405)

*Explanation of "Freedom from Extremes through Understanding All Tenets": Ocean of Eloquence*

grub mtha' kun shes nas mtha' bral grub pa zhes bya ba'i bstan bcos rnam par bshad pa legs bshad kyi rgya mtsho

Thimphu, Bhutan: Kun-bzang-stobs rgyal, 1976.

Döl-b̄o-b̄a Ṡhay-rap-gyel-tsen (*dol po pa shes rab rgyal mtshan,* 1292-1361)

*Great Calculation of the Doctrine, Which Has the Significance of a Fourth Council*

bka' bsdu bzhi pa'i don bstan rtsis chen po

Matthew Kapstein. *The 'Dzam-thang Edition of the Collected Works of Kun-mkhyen Dol-po-pa Shes-rab-rgyal-mtshan: Introduction and Catalogue,* vol. 5, 207-252. Delhi: Shedrup Books, 1992.

English translation: Cyrus R. Stearns. *The Buddha from Dolpo: A Study of the Life and Thought of the Tibetan Master Dolpopa Sherab Gyaltsen,* 127-173. Albany, N.Y.: State University of New York Press, 1999.

*Mountain Doctrine, Ocean of Definitive Meaning: Final Unique Quintessential Instructions*

ri chos nges don rgya mtsho zhes bya ba mthar thug thun mong ma yin pa'i man ngag

Gangtok, India: Dodrup Sangyey Lama, 1976.

Also: 'dzam thang bsam 'grub nor bu'i gling, n.d.

Also: Matthew Kapstein. *The 'Dzam-thang Edition of the Collected Works of Kun-mkhyen Dol-po-pa Shes-rab-rgyal-mtshan: Introduction and Catalogue,* vol. 2, 25-707. Delhi: Shedrup Books, 1992.

Also: Beijing: mi rigs dpe skrun khang, 1998.

English translation: Jeffrey Hopkins. *Mountain Doctrine: Tibet's Fundamental Treatise on Other-Emptiness and the Buddha Matrix.* Ithaca, N.Y.: Snow Lion Publications, 2006.

*Eloquent Elucidation of (Maitreya's) "Treatise on the Sublime Continuum": Rays of the Sun*

theg pa chen po rgyud bla ma'i bstan bcos legs bshad nyi ma'i 'od zer

Thimphu, Bhutan: Kunsang Topgay, 1976.

*[Interlinear Commentary on Nāgārjuna's] "Praise of the Element of Attributes"*

'phags pa klu sgrub kyis mdzad pa'i chos dbyings bstod pa

*Collected Works*, vol. *e*, 141-161. N.p., n.d.

D̄zong-ka-b̄a L̄o-sang-drak-b̄a (*tsong kha pa blo bzang grags pa*, 1357-1419)

*Extensive Explanation of (Chandrakīrti's) "Supplement to (Nāgārjuna's) 'Treatise on the Middle'": Illumination of the Thought*

dbu ma la 'jug pa'i rgya cher bshad pa dgongs pa rab gsal

P6143, vol. 154. Also: Sarnath, India: Pleasure of Elegant Sayings Press, 1973. Also: Delhi: Ngawang Gelek, 1975. Also: Delhi: Guru Deva, 1979.

English translation (chapters 1-5): Jeffrey Hopkins. *Compassion in Tibetan Buddhism*, 93-230. Ithaca, N.Y.: Snow Lion Publications, 1980.

English translation (chap. 6, stanzas 1-7): Jeffrey Hopkins and Anne C. Klein. *Path to the Middle: Madhyamaka Philosophy in Tibet: The Oral Scholarship of Kensur Yeshay Tupden*, by Anne C. Klein, 147-183, 252-271. Albany, N.Y.: State University of New York Press, 1994.

*Great Exposition of the Stages of the Path / Stages of the Path to Enlightenment Thoroughly Teaching All the Stages of Practice of the Three Types of Beings*

lam rim chen mo / skyes bu gsum gyi nyams su blang ba'i rim pa thams cad tshang bar ston pa'i byang chub lam gyi rim pa

P6001, vol. 152. Also: Dharamsala, India: Tibetan Cultural Printing Press, 1964. Also: Delhi: Ngawang Gelek, 1975. Also: Delhi: Guru Deva, 1979.

English translation: Tsong-kha-pa. *The Great Treatise on the Stages of the Path to Enlightenment.* 3 vols. Trans. and ed. Joshua W. C. Cutler and Guy Newland. Ithaca, N.Y.: Snow Lion Publications, 2000-2003.

English translation of the part on the excessively broad object of negation: Elizabeth Napper. *Dependent-Arising and Emptiness*, 153-215. London: Wisdom Publications, 1989.

English translation of the parts on calm abiding and special insight: Alex Wayman. *Calming the Mind and Discerning the Real*, 81-431. New York: Columbia University Press, 1978; reprint, New Delhi: Motilal Banarsidass, 1979.

*Treatise Differentiating the Interpretable and the Definitive: The Essence of Eloquence*

drang ba dang nges pa'i don rnam par phye ba'i bstan bcos legs bshad snying po

Editions: see the preface to my critical edition, *Emptiness in the Mind-Only School of Buddhism*, 355. Also: Ye shes thabs mkhas. *shar tsong kha pa blo bzang grags pas mdzad pa'i drang ba dang nges pa'i don rnam par phye ba'i bstan bcos legs bshad snying po.* Tā la'i bla ma'i 'phags bod, vol. 22. Varanasi, India: vāṇa dbus bod kyi ches mtho'i gtsug lag slob gnyer khang, 1997.

English translation: Prologue and Mind-Only section, *Emptiness in the Mind-Only School of Buddhism, Dynamic Responses to Dzong-ka-ba's* The Essence of Eloquence, volume 1. Berkeley: University of California Press, 1999; Delhi: Munshiram Manoharlal, 2000. Also: Robert A. F. Thurman. *Tsong Khapa's Speech of Gold in the Essence of True Eloquence*, 185-385. Princeton, N.J.: Princeton University Press, 1984.

Chinese translation: Venerable Fa Zun. "Bian Liao Yi Bu Liao Yi Shuo Cang Lun." In *Xi Zang Fo Jiao Jiao Yi Lun Ji*, 2, 159-276. Taipei: Da Sheng Wen Hua Chu Ban She, 1979.

Ge-dün-gya-tso, Second Dalai Lama (*dge 'dun rgya mtsho*, 1476-1542)

*Ship for Entering the Ocean of Tenets*

grub mtha' rgya mtshor 'jug pa'i gru rdzings

Varaṇāsi: Ye shes stobs ldan, 1969

Ḡön-chok-jik-may-w̄ang-b̄o (*dkon mchog 'jigs med dbang po*, 1728-1791)

*Precious Garland of Tenets / Presentation of Tenets: A Precious Garland* grub pa'i mtha'i rnam par bzhag pa rin po che'i phreng ba

Tibetan: K. Mimaki. "Le Grub mtha' rnam bzhag rin chen phreṅ ba de dkon mchog 'jigs med dbaṅ po (1728-1791)," *Zinbun* [The Research Institute for Humanistic Studies, Kyoto University], 14 (1977): 55-112. Also, *Collected Works of dkon-mchog-'jigs-med-dbaṅ-po*, vol. 6, 485-535. New Delhi: Ngawang Gelek Demo, 1972. Also: Xylograph in thirty-two folios from the Lessing Collection of the rare book section of the University of Wisconsin Library, which is item 47 in Leonard Zwilling. *Tibetan Blockprints in the Department of Rare Books and Special Collections*. Madison, Wis.: University of Wisconsin-Madison Libraries, 1984. Also: Mundgod, India: blo gsal gling Press, 1980. Also: Dharamsala, India: Tibetan Cultural Printing Press, 1967. Also: Dharamsala, India: Teaching Training, n.d. Also: A blockprint edition in twenty-eight folios obtained in 1987 from Go-mang College in Hla-s̄a, printed on blocks that predate the Cultural Revolution.

English translation: Geshe Lhundup Sopa and Jeffrey Hopkins. *Practice and Theory of Tibetan Buddhism*, 48-145. New York: Grove, 1976; rev. ed., *Cutting through Appearances: Practice and Theory of Tibetan Buddhism*, 109-322. Ithaca, N.Y.: Snow Lion Publications, 1989. Also: H. V. Guenther. *Buddhist Philosophy in Theory and Practice*. Baltimore, Md.: Penguin, 1972. Also, the chapters on the Autonomy School and the Consequence School: Shōtarō Iida. *Reason and Emptiness*, 27-51. Tokyo: Hokuseido, 1980.

Haribhadra (*seng ge bzang po*, late eighth century)

*Clear Meaning Commentary / Commentary on (Maitreya's) "Ornament for Clear Realization, Treatise of Quintessential Instructions on the Perfection of Wisdom"*

sphuṭhārtha / abhisamayālaṃkāranāmaprajñāpāramitopadeśaśāstravṛtti

'grel pa don gsal / shes rab kyi pha rol tu phyin pa'i man ngag gi bstan bcos mngon par rtogs pa'i rgyan ces bya ba'i 'grel pa

P5191, vol. 90

Sanskrit: Unrai Wogihara. *Abhisamayālaṃkārālokā Prajñā-pāramitā-vyākhyā, The Work of Haribhadra*. 7 vols. Tokyo: Toyo Bunko, 1932-1935; reprint, Tokyo: Sankibo Buddhist Book Store, 1973.

*Illumination of the Eight Thousand Stanza Perfection of Wisdom Sūtra*

āryāṣṭasāhasrikāprajñāpāramitāvyākhyānābhisamayālaṃkārāloka-nāma

'phags pa shes rab kyi pha rol tu phyin pa brgyad stong pa'i bshad pa mngon par rtogs pa'i rgyan gyi snang ba zhes bya ba

P 5189, vol.90

Sanskrit: Unrai Wogihara. *Abhisamayālaṃkārālokā Prajñā-pāramitā-vyākhyā, The Work of Haribhadra*. 7 vols. Tokyo: Toyo Bunko, 1932-1935; reprint, Tokyo: Sankibo Buddhist Book Store, 1973; and P. L. Vaidya. *Aṣṭasāhasrika Prajñāpāramitā, with Haribhadra's Commentary called Ālokā*. Buddhist Sanskrit Texts 4. Darbhanga, India: Mithila Institute, 1960.

English translation: E. Conze. *The Perfection of Wisdom in Eight Thousand Lines & Its Verse Summary*. Bolinas, Calif.: Four Seasons Foundation, 1973.

Jam-ȳang-shay-b̄a Nga-w̄ang-d̄zön-drü (*'jam dbyangs bzhad pa ngag dbang brtson grus*, 1648-1722)

*Great Exposition of Tenets / Explanation of "Tenets": Sun of the Land of Samantabhadra Brilliantly Illuminating All of Our Own and Others' Tenets and the Meaning of the Profound [Emptiness], Ocean of Scripture and Reasoning Fulfilling All Hopes of All Beings*

grub mtha' chen mo / grub mtha'i rnam bshad rang gzhan grub mtha' kun dang zab don mchog tu gsal ba kun bzang zhing gi nyi ma lung rigs rgya mtsho skye dgu'i re ba kun skong

Edition cited: Musoorie, India: Dalama, 1962. Also: *Collected Works of 'Jam-dbyaṅs-bźad-pa'i-rdo-rje*, vol. 14 (entire). New Delhi: Ngawang Gelek Demo, 1973. Also: Mundgod, India: Drepung Gomang Library, 1999.

English translation (entire root text and edited portions of the autocommentary and Nga-w̄ang-b̄el-den's *Annotations*): Jeffrey Hopkins. *Maps of the Profound: Jam-yang-shay-ba's Great Exposition of Buddhist and Non-Buddhist Views on the Nature of Reality*. Ithaca, N.Y.: Snow Lion Publications, 2003.

English translation (beginning of the chapter on the Consequence School): Jeffrey Hopkins. *Meditation on Emptiness*, 581-697. London: Wisdom, 1983; rev. ed., Boston: Wisdom, 1996.

J̄ang-ḡya Röl-b̄ay-dor-jay (*lcang skya rol pa'i rdo rje*, 1717-1786)

*Presentations of Tenets / Clear Exposition of the Presentations of Tenets: Beautiful Ornament for the Meru of the Subduer's Teaching*

grub mtha'i rnam bzhag / grub pa'i mtha'i rnam par bzhag pa gsal bar bshad pa thub bstan lhun po'i mdzes rgyan

Edition cited: Varanasi, India: Pleasure of Elegant Sayings Printing Press, 1970. Also: Lokesh Chandra, ed. *Buddhist Philosophical Systems of Lcaṅ-skya Rol-pahi Rdo-rje*. Śata-piṭaka Series (Indo-Asian Literatures), vol. 233. New Delhi: International Academy of Indian Culture, 1977. Also: An edition published by gam car phan bde legs bshad gling grva tshang dang rgyud rnying slar gso tshogs pa, 1982.

English translation of Sautrāntika chapter: Anne C. Klein. *Knowing, Naming, and Negation*, 115-196. Ithaca, N.Y.: Snow Lion Publications, 1988. Commentary on this: Anne C. Klein. *Knowledge and Liberation: A Buddhist Epistemological Analysis in Support of Transformative Religious Experience*. Ithaca, N.Y.: Snow Lion Publications, 1986.

English translation of Svātantrika chapter: Donald S. Lopez Jr. *A Study of Svātantrika*, 243-386. Ithaca, N.Y.: Snow Lion Publications, 1986.

English translation of part of Prāsaṅgika chapter: Jeffrey Hopkins. *Emptiness Yoga: The Tibetan Middle Way*, 355-428. Ithaca, N.Y.: Snow Lion Publications, 1983.

Jay-d̄zün Chö-ḡyi-gyel-tsen (*rje btsun chos kyi rgyal mtshan*, 1469-1546)

*Presentation of Tenets*

grub mtha'i rnam gzhag

Buxaduor, India: n.p., 1960. Also: Bylakuppe, India: Se-ra Byes Monastery, 1977.

L̄ong-chen-rap-jam (*klong chen rab 'byams / klong chen dri med 'od zer*, 1308-1363)

*Precious Treasury of Tenets: Illuminating the Meaning of All Vehicles*

theg pa mtha' dag gi don gsal bar byed pa grub pa'i mtha' rin po che'i mdzod

Gangtok, Sikkim: Dodrup Chen Rinpoche, 1969[?].

Maitreya (*byams pa*)

**Five Doctrines of Maitreya**

1. *Sublime Continuum of the Great Vehicle / Treatise on the Later Scriptures of the Great Vehicle*

mahāyānottaratantraśāstra

theg pa chen po rgyud bla ma'i bstan bcos

P5525, vol. 108

Sanskrit: E. H. Johnston (and T. Chowdhury). *The Ratnagotravibhāga Mahāyānottaratantraśāstra*. Patna, India: Bihar Research Society, 1950.

English translation: E. Obermiller. "Sublime Science of the Great Vehicle to Salvation." *Acta Orientalia* 9 (1931): 81-306. Also: J. Takasaki. *A Study on the*

*Ratnagotravibhāga.* Serie Orientale Roma 33. Rome: Istituto Italiano per il Medio ed Estremo Oriente, 1966.

2. *Differentiation of Phenomena and Noumenon*
dharmadharmatāvibhaṅga
chos dang chos nyid rnam par 'byed pa
P5523, vol. 108
Edited Tibetan: Jōshō Nozawa. "The *Dharmadharmatāvibhaṅga* and the *Dharmadharmatā-vibhaṅgavṛtti,* Tibetan Texts, Edited and Collated, Based upon the Peking and Derge Editions." In *Studies in Indology and Buddhology: Presented in Honour of Professor Susumu Yamaguchi on the Occasion of his Sixtieth Birthday,* edited by Gadjin M. Nagao and Jōshō Nozawa. Kyoto: Hozokan, 1955.
English translation: John Younghan Cha. "A Study of the *Dharmadharmatāvibhāga:* An Analysis of the Religious Philosophy of the Yogācāra, Together with an Annotated Translation of Vasubandhu's Commentary." Ph.D. diss., Northwestern University, 1996.
English translation: Jim Scott. *Maitreya's Distinguishing Phenomena and Pure Being with Commentary by Mipham.* Ithaca, N.Y.: Snow Lion Publications, 2004.

3. *Differentiation of the Middle and the Extremes*
madhyāntavibhaṅga
dbus dang mtha' rnam par 'byed pa
P5522, vol. 108
Sanskrit: Gadjin M. Nagao. *Madhyāntavibhāga-bhāṣya.* Tokyo: Suzuki Research Foundation, 1964. Also: Ramchandra Pandeya. *Madhyānta-vibhāga-śāstra.* Delhi: Motilal Banarsidass, 1971.
English translation: Stefan Anacker. *Seven Works of Vasubandhu.* Delhi: Motilal Banarsidass, 1984. Also, of chapter 1: Thomas A. Kochumuttom. *A Buddhist Doctrine of Experience.* Delhi: Motilal Banarsidass, 1982. Also, of chapter 1: Th. Stcherbatsky. *Madhyāntavibhāga, Discourse on Discrimination between Middle and Extremes Ascribed to Bodhisattva Maitreya and Commented by Vasubandhu and Sthiramati.* Bibliotheca Buddhica 30 (1936). Osnabrück, Germany: Biblio Verlag, 1970; reprint, Calcutta: Indian Studies Past and Present, 1971. Also, of chapter 1: David Lasar Friedmann. *Sthiramati, Madhyāntavibhāgaṭīkā: Analysis of the Middle Path and the Extremes.* Utrecht, Netherlands: Rijksuniversiteit te Leiden, 1937.

4. *Ornament for Clear Realization*
abhisamayālaṃkāra
mngon par rtogs pa'i rgyan
P5184, vol. 88
Sanskrit: Th. Stcherbatsky and E. Obermiller, eds. *Abhisamayālaṃkāra-Prajñāpāramitā-Upadeśa-Śāstra.* Bibliotheca Buddhica 23. Osnabrück, Germany: Biblio Verlag, 1970.
English translation: Edward Conze. *Abhisamayālaṃkāra.* Serie Orientale Roma 6. Rome: Istituto Italiano per il Medio ed Estremo Oriente, 1954.

5. *Ornament for the Great Vehicle Sūtras*
mahāyānasūtrālaṃkāra
theg pa chen po'i mdo sde rgyan gyi tshig le'ur byas pa
P5521, vol. 108
Sanskrit: Sitansusekhar Bagchi. *Mahāyāna-Sūtrālaṃkāraḥ of Asaṅga* [with Vasubandhu's commentary]. Buddhist Sanskrit Texts 13. Darbhanga, India: Mithila Institute, 1970.

Sanskrit text and translation into French: Sylvain Lévi. *Mahāyānasūtrālaṃkāra, exposé de la doctrine du grand véhicule selon le système Yogācāra.* Bibliothèque de l'École des Hautes Études. 2 vols. Paris: Libraire Honoré Champion, 1907, 1911.

Sanskrit text and translation into English: Surekha Vijay Limaye. *Mahāyānasūtrālaṃkāra by Asaṅga.* Bibliotheca Indo-Buddhica Series 94. Delhi: Sri Satguru, 1992.

English translation: L. Jamspal et al. *The Universal Vehicle Discourse Literature.* Editor-in-chief, Robert A.F Thurman. New York: American Institute of Buddhist Studies, Columbia University, 2004.

Nāgārjuna (*klu sgrub,* first to second century, C.E.)

*Praise of the Element of Attributes*

dharmadhātustotra

chos kyi dbyings su bstod pa

P2010, vol.46; Toh. 1118, vol. ka

**Six Collections of Reasonings**

1. *Precious Garland of Advice for the King*

rājaparikathāratnāvalī

rgyal po la gtam bya ba rin po che'i phreng ba

P5658, vol. 129

Sanskrit, Tibetan, and Chinese: Michael Hahn. *Nāgārjuna's Ratnāvalī,* vol. 1. *The Basic Texts (Sanskrit, Tibetan, and Chinese).* Bonn: Indica et Tibetica Verlag, 1982.

English translation: Jeffrey Hopkins. *Buddhist Advice for Living and Liberation: Nāgārjuna's Precious Garland,* 94-164. Ithaca, N.Y.: Snow Lion Publications, 1998. Supersedes that in: Nāgārjuna and the Seventh Dalai Lama. *The Precious Garland and the Song of the Four Mindfulnesses,* translated by Jeffrey Hopkins, 17-93. London: George Allen and Unwin, 1975; New York: Harper and Row, 1975; reprint, in H.H. the Dalai Lama, Tenzin Gyatso. *The Buddhism of Tibet.* London: George Allen and Unwin, 1983; reprint, Ithaca, N.Y.: Snow Lion Publications, 1987.

English translation: John Dunne and Sara McClintock. *The Precious Garland: An Epistle to a King.* Boston: Wisdom Publications, 1997.

English translation of chap. 1, 1-77: Giuseppe Tucci. "The *Ratnāvalī* of Nāgārjuna." *Journal of the Royal Asiatic Society* (1934): 307-324; reprint, Giuseppe Tucci. *Opera Minora,* II. Rome: Giovanni Bardi Editore, 1971, 321-366. Chap. 2, 1-46; chap. 4, 1-100: Giuseppe Tucci. "The *Ratnāvalī* of Nāgārjuna." *Journal of the Royal Asiatic Society* (1936): 237-252, 423-435.

Japanese translation: Uryūzu Ryushin. *Butten II, Sekai Koten Bungaku Zenshu,* 7 (July, 1965): 349-372. Edited by Nakamura Hajime. Tokyo: Chikuma Shobō. Also: Uryūzu Ryushin. *Daijō Butten* 14 (1974): 231-316. *Ryūju Ronshū.* Edited by Kajiyama Yuichi and Uryūzu Ryushin. Tokyo: Chūōkōronsha.

Danish translation: Christian Lindtner. *Nagarjuna, Juvelkaeden og andre skrifter.* Copenhagen, 1980.

2. *Refutation of Objections*

vigrahavyāvartanīkārikā

rtsod pa bzlog pa'i tshig le'ur byas pa

P5228, vol. 95

Edited Tibetan and Sanskrit: Christian Lindtner. *Nagarjuniana,* 70-86. Indiske Studier 4. Copenhagen: Akademisk Forlag, 1982.

Edited Sanskrit and English translation: K. Bhattacharya, E. H. Johnston, and A. Kunst. *The Dialectical Method of Nāgārjuna.* New Delhi: Motilal Banarsidass, 1978.

English translation from the Chinese: G. Tucci. *Pre-Diṅnāga Buddhist Texts on Logic from Chinese Sources.* Gaekwad's Oriental Series 49. Baroda, India: Oriental Institute, 1929.

French translation: S. Yamaguchi. "Traité de Nāgārjuna pour écarter les vaines discussion (Vigrahavyāvartanī) traduit et annoté." *Journal Asiatique* 215 (1929): 1-86.

3. *Seventy Stanzas on Emptiness*
śūnyatāsaptatikārikā
stong pa nyid bdun cu pa'i tshig le'ur byas pa
P5227, vol. 95
Edited Tibetan and English translation: Christian Lindtner. *Nagarjuniana,* 34-69. Indiske Studier 4. Copenhagen: Akademisk Forlag, 1982.
English translation: David Ross Komito. *Nāgārjuna's "Seventy Stanzas": A Buddhist Psychology of Emptiness.* Ithaca, N.Y.: Snow Lion Publications, 1987.

4. *Sixty Stanzas of Reasoning*
yuktiṣaṣṭikākārikā
rigs pa drug cu pa'i tshig le'ur byas pa
P5225, vol. 95
Edited Tibetan with Sanskrit fragments and English translation: Christian Lindtner. *Nagarjuniana,* 100-119. Indiske Studier 4. Copenhagen: Akademisk Forlag, 1982.

5. *Treatise Called the Finely Woven*
vaidalyasūtranāma
zhib mo rnam par 'thag pa zhes bya ba'i mdo
P5226, vol. 95
Tibetan text and English translation: Fernando Tola and Carmen Dragonetti. *Nāgārjuna's Refutation of Logic (Nyāya) Vaidalyaprakaraṇa.* Delhi: Motilal Banarsidass, 1995.

6. *Treatise on the Middle / Fundamental Treatise on the Middle, Called "Wisdom"*
madhyamakaśāstra / prajñānāmamūlamadhyamakakārikā
dbu ma'i bstan bcos / dbu ma rtsa ba'i tshig le'ur byas pa shes rab ces bya ba
P5224, vol. 95
Edited Sanskrit: J. W. de Jong. *Nāgārjuna, Mūlamadhyamakakārikāḥ.* Madras, India: Adyar Library and Research Centre, 1977; reprint, Wheaton, Ill.: Theosophical Publishing House, c. 1977. Also: Christian Lindtner. *Nāgārjuna's Filosofiske Vaerker,* 177-215. Indiske Studier 2. Copenhagen: Akademisk Forlag, 1982.
English translation: Frederick Streng. *Emptiness: A Study in Religious Meaning.* Nashville, Tenn.: Abingdon Press, 1967. Also: Kenneth Inada. *Nāgārjuna: A Translation of His Mūlamadhyamakakārikā.* Tokyo: Hokuseido Press, 1970. Also: David J. Kalupahana. *Nāgārjuna: The Philosophy of the Middle Way.* Albany, N.Y.: State University of New York Press, 1986. Also: Jay L. Garfield. *The Fundamental Wisdom of the Middle Way.* New York: Oxford University Press, 1995.
Italian translation: R. Gnoli. *Nāgārjuna: Madhyamaka Kārikā, Le stanze del cammino di mezzo.* Enciclopedia di autori classici 61. Turin, Italy: P. Boringhieri, 1961.
Danish translation: Christian Lindtner. *Nāgārjuna's Filosofiske Vaerker,* 67-135. Indiske Studier 2. Copenhagen: Akademisk Forlag, 1982.

Nga-w̄ang-b̄el-den (*ngag dbang dpal ldan,* b. 1797), also known as B̄el-den-chö-jay (*dpal ldan chos rje*)

*Annotations for (Jam-ȳang-shay-b̄a's) "Great Exposition of Tenets": Freeing the Knots of the Difficult Points, Precious Jewel of Clear Thought*
grub mtha' chen mo'i mchan 'grel dka' gnad mdud grol blo gsal gces nor

Sarnath, India: Pleasure of Elegant Sayings Press, 1964. Also: *Collected Works of Chos-rje ṅag-dbaṅ Dpal-ldan of Urga,* vols. 4 (entire)-5, 1-401. Delhi: Guru Deva, 1983.

Paṇ-chen Sö-nam-drak-b̄a (*paṇ chen bsod nams grags pa,* 1478-1554)

*Presentation of Tenets: Sublime Tree Inspiring Those of Clear Mind, Hammer Destroying the Stone Mountains of Opponents*

grub mtha'i rnam bzhag blo gsal spro ba bskyed pa'i ljon pa phas rgol brag ri 'joms pa'i tho ba

Buxa, n.d.

Puṇḍarīka, Kalkī (*rigs ldan pad ma dkar po*)

*Great Commentary on the "Kālachakra Tantra": Stainless Light*

vimālaprabhānāmamūlatantrānusāriṇīdvādaśasāhasrikālaghukālacakratantrarājaṭīkā

bsdus pa'i rgyud kyi rgyal po dus kyi 'khor lo'i 'grel bshad rtsa ba'i rgyud kyi rjes su 'jug pa stong phrag bcu gnyis pa dri ma med pa'i 'od ces bya ba

P2064, vol. 46

English translation of the first section: John Newman. "The Outer Wheel of Time: Vajrayāna Buddhist Cosmology in the Kālachakra Tantra." Ph.D. dissertation, Univ. of Wisconsin, 1987.

Shāntarakṣhita (*śāntarakṣita, zhi ba 'tsho,* eighth century)

*Compendium of Principles*

tattvasaṃgrahakārikā

de kho na nyid bsdud pa'i tshig le'ur byas pa

P5764, vol. 138

Sanskrit: Dwarikadas Shastri. *Tattvasaṅgraha of Ācārya Shāntarakṣita, with the Commentary "Pañjikā" of Shrī Kamalạshīla.* Varanasi, India: Bauddha Bharati, 1968.

English translation: G. Jha. *The Tattvasaṃgraha of Śāntarakṣita, with the commentary of Kamalaśīla.* Gaekwad's Oriental Series 80 and 83. Baroda, India: Oriental Institute, 1937, 1939; reprint, Delhi: Motilal Barnarsidass, 1986.

Tāranātha (1575-1634)

*Essence of Ambrosia*

rgyal ba'i bstan pa la 'jug pa'i rim pa skyes bu gsum gyi man ngag gi khrid yig bdud rtsi'i snying khu

*Collected Works of Jo-naṅ rJe-btsun Tāranātha,* vol. 18 (*tsha*), 241-333. Dzamthang Monastery, Aba Prefecture, Sichuan Province, 1990s.

English translation: Willa Baker. *Essence of Ambrosia.* Dharamsala, India: Library of Tibetan Works and Archives, 2005.

*The Essence of Other-Emptiness*

gzhan stong snying po

*Collected Works of Jo-naṅ rJe-btsun Tāranātha,* vol. 4 (*nga*), 491-514. Leh, Ladakh: Smanrtsis Shesrig Dpemzod, 1985. Also, vol. 18 (*tsha*), 171-193. Dzamthang Monastery, Aba Prefecture, Sichuan Province, 1990s.

*History of Buddhism in India/ Clear Teaching of How the Precious Holy Doctrine Spread in the Land of Superiors [India], Fulfilling All Needs and Wishes*

rgya gar chos 'byung/ dam pa'i chos rin po che 'phags pa'i yul du ji ltar dar ba'i tshul gsal bar ston pa dgos 'dod kun 'byung

Sarnath: Pleasure of Elegant Sayings Press, 1972

Russian translation: V.P. Vasil'ev. St. Petersburg: April, 1869.

German translation: Anton Schieffer. *Geschichte des Buddhismus in Indien.* St. Petersburg: October, 1869.

English translation: E. Obermiller. *History of Buddhism (Chos-ḥbyung) by Bu-ston.*

Heidelberg: O. Harrassowitz, 1931-1932; reprint, Tokyo: Suzuki Research Foundation, n.d. Also: Lama Chimpa, and Alaka Chattopadhyaya. *Tāranātha's History of Buddhism in India.* Simla, India: Indian Institute of Advanced Study, 1970; reprint, Delhi: Motilal Banarsidass, 1990.

*Long History of the Yamāntaka-Tantra-Rāja Cycle [Called "Causing] Wondrous Belief"*
rgyud rgyal gshin rje gshed skor gyi chos 'byung rgyas pa yid ches ngo mtshar
*Collected Works of Jo-naṅ rJe-btsun Tāranātha,* vol. 10. Leh, Ladakh: Smanrtsis Shesrig Dpemzod, 1985.
Unpublished English translation by Gareth Sparham.

*Ornament of the Other-Empty Middle*
gzhan stong dbu ma'i rgyan
*Collected Works of Jo-naṅ rJe-btsun Tāranātha,* vol. 4 (*nga*), 797-824. Leh, Ladakh: Smanrtsis Shesrig Dpemzod, 1985

*Story of the Lineage Endowed with Seven Transmissions*
bka' babs bdun ldan gyi brgyud pa'i rnam thar
English translation: David Templeman, *Tāranātha's Bka' babs bdun ldan: The Seven Instruction Lineages.* Dharamsala, India: Library of Tibetan Works and Archives, 1983.

*Twenty-one Differences Regarding the Profound Meaning*
zab don gnyer gcig pa
*Collected Works of Jo-naṅ rJe-btsun Tāranātha,* vol. 4 (*nga*), 781-794. Leh, Ladakh: Smanrtsis Shesrig Dpemzod, 1985. Also, vol. 18 (*tsha*), 209-222. Dzamthang Monastery, Aba Prefecture, Sichuan Province, 1990s.
English translation: Klaus-Dieter Mathes. "Tāranātha's Twenty-one Differences with Regard to the Profound Meaning." *Journal of the International Association of Buddhist Studies,* vol. 27, no. 2 (2004): 285-328.

Vasubandhu (*dbyig gnyen,* fl. 360)

*[Commentary on] the Three Mothers: Conquest over Harm / Extensive Explanation of the Superior One Hundred Thousand Stanza, Twenty-five Thousand Stanza, and Eighteen Thousand Stanza Perfection of Wisdom Sūtras / Commentary on the Extensive and Middling Mothers*
āryaśatasāhasrikāpañcaviṃsatisāhasrikāṣṭadaśasāhasrikāprajñāpāramitābṛhaṭṭīkā
yum gsum gnod 'joms / 'phags pa shes rab kyi pha rol tu phyin pa 'bum pa dang nyi khri lnga stong pa dang khri brgyad stong pa'i rgya cher bshad pa
P5206, vol. 93

*Commentary on (Maitreya's) "Differentiation of Phenomena and Noumenon"*
dharmadharmatāvibhāgavṛtti
chos dang chos nyid rnam par 'byed pa'i 'grel pa
P5529, vol. 108
Edited Tibetan: Jōshō Nozawa. "The *Dharmadharmatāvibhaṅga* and the *Dharmadharmatā-vibhaṅgavṛtti,* Tibetan Texts, Edited and Collated, Based upon the Peking and Derge Editions." In *Studies in Indology and Buddhology: Presented in Honour of Professor Susumu Yamaguchi on the Occasion of his Sixtieth Birthday,* edited by Gadjin M. Nagao and Jōshō Nozawa. Kyoto: Hozokan, 1955.
English translation: John Younghan Cha. A Study of the *Dharmadharmatāvibhāga:* An Analysis of the Religious Philosophy of the Yogācāra, Together with an Annotated Translation of Vasubandhu's Commentary. Ph.D. diss., Northwestern University, 1996.

**Eight Prakaraṇa Treatises**

1. *Commentary on (Maitreya's) "Differentiation of the Middle and the Extremes"*
madhyāntavibhāgaṭīkā
dbus dang mtha' rnam par 'byed pa'i 'grel pa / dbus mtha'i 'grel pa
P5528, vol. 108
Sanskrit: Gadjin M. Nagao. *Madhyāntavibhāga-bhāṣya.* Tokyo: Suzuki Research Foundation, 1964. Also: Ramchandra Pandeya. *Madhyānta-vibhāga-śāstra.* Delhi: Motilal Banarsidass, 1971.
English translation: Stefan Anacker. *Seven Works of Vasubandhu.* Delhi: Motilal Banarsidass, 1984. Also: Thomas A. Kochumuttom. *A Buddhist Doctrine of Experience.* Delhi: Motilal Banarsidass, 1982. Also, of chapter 1: Th. Stcherbatsky. *Madhyānta-vibhāga: Discourse on Discrimination between Middle and Extremes Ascribed to Bodhisattva Maitreya and Commented by Vasubandhu and Sthiramati.* Bibliotheca Buddhica 30 (1936). Osnabrück, Germany: Biblio Verlag, 1970; reprint, Calcutta: Indian Studies Past and Present, 1971. Also, of chapter 1: David Lasar Friedmann, *Sthiramati, Madhyāntavibhāgaṭīkā: Analysis of the Middle Path and the Extremes.* Utrecht, Netherlands: Rijksuniversiteit te Leiden, 1937.
2. *Explanation of (Maitreya's) "Ornament for the Great Vehicle Sūtras"*
sūtrālaṃkārābhāṣya
mdo sde'i rgyan gyi bshad pa
P5527, vol. 108
Sanskrit: S. Bagchi. *Mahāyāna-Sūtrālaṃkāra of Asaṅga* [with Vasubandhu's commentary]. Buddhist Sanskrit Texts 13. Darbhanga, India: Mithila Institute, 1970.
Sanskrit and translation into French: Sylvain Lévi. *Mahāyānasūtrālaṃkāra, exposé de la doctrine du grand véhicule selon le système Yogācāra.* 2 vols. Paris: Libraire Honoré Champion, 1907, 1911.
English translation: L. Jamspal et al. *The Universal Vehicle Discourse Literature.* Editor-in-chief, Robert A.F Thurman. New York: American Institute of Buddhist Studies, Columbia University, 2004.
3. *Principles of Explanation*
vyākyhayukti
rnam par bshad pa'i rigs pa
P5562, vol. 113
4. *The Thirty / Treatise on Cognition-Only in Thirty Stanzas*
triṃśikākārikā / sarvavijñānamātradeśakatriṃśakakārikā
sum cu pa'i tshig le'ur byas pa / thams cad rnam rig tsam du ston pa sum cu pa'i tshig le'ur byas pa
P5556, vol. 113
Sanskrit: Sylvain Lévi. *Vijñaptimātratāsiddhi / Deux traités de Vasubandhu: Viṃśatikā (La Vingtaine) et Triṃsikā (La Trentaine).* Bibliothèque de l'École des Hautes Études. Paris: Libraire Honoré Champion, 1925. Also: K. N. Chatterjee. *Vijñapti-Mātratā-Siddhi (with Sthiramati's Commentary).* Varanasi, India: Kishor Vidya Niketan, 1980.
English translation: Stefan Anacker. *Seven Works of Vasubandhu.* Delhi: Motilal Banarsidass, 1984. Also: Thomas A. Kochumuttom. *A Buddhist Doctrine of Experience.* Delhi: Motilal Banarsidass, 1982.
5. *Treasury of Manifest Knowledge*
abhidharmakośakārikā
chos mngon pa'i mdzod kyi tshig le'ur byas pa

P5590, vol. 115

Sanskrit: Swami Dwarikadas Shastri. *Abhidharmakośa & Bhāṣya of Ācārya Vasubandhu with Sphuṭārtha Commentary of Ācārya Yaśomitra.* Bauddha Bharati Series 5. Banaras, India: Bauddha Bharati, 1970. Also: P. Pradhan. *Abhidharmakośabhāṣyam of Vasubandhu.* Patna, India: Jayaswal Research Institute, 1975.

French translation: Louis de La Vallée Poussin. *L'Abhidharmakośa de Vasubandhu.* 6 vols. Brussels: Institut Belge des Hautes Études Chinoises, 1971.

English translation of the French: Leo M. Pruden. *Abhidharmakośabhāṣyam.* 4 vols. Berkeley, Calif.: Asian Humanities Press, 1988.

6. *The Twenty*

vimśatikā / vimśikākārikā

nyi shu pa'i tshig le'ur byas pa

P5557, vol. 113

Sanskrit: Sylvain Lévi. *Vijñaptimātratāsiddhi / Deux traités de Vasubandhu: Vimśatikā (La Vingtaine) et Trimsikā (La Trentaine).* Bibliotheque de l'École des Hautes Études. Paris: Libraire Honoré Champion, 1925.

English translation: Stefan Anacker. *Seven Works of Vasubandhu.* Delhi: Motilal Banarsidass, 1984. Also: Thomas A. Kochumuttom. *A Buddhist Doctrine of Experience.* Delhi: Motilal Banarsidass, 1982.

English translation (stanzas 1-10): Gregory A. Hillis. "An Introduction and Translation of Vinītadeva's Explanation of the First Ten Stanzas of [Vasubandhu's] Commentary on His 'Twenty Stanzas,' with Appended Glossary of Technical Terms." M.A. thesis, University of Virginia, 1993.

7. *Work on Achieving Actions*

karmasiddhiprakaraṇa

las grub pa'i rab tu byed pa

P5563, vol. 113

French translation (chap. 17): É. Lamotte. "Le Traité de l'acte de Vasubandhu, Karmasiddhiprakaraṇa." *Mélanges Chinois et Bouddhiques* 4 (1936): 265-288.

8. *Work on the Five Aggregates*

pañcaskandhaprakaraṇa

phung po lnga'i rab tu byed pa

P5560, vol. 113

W̄el-mang Ḡön-chok-gyel-tsen (*dbal mang dkon mchog rgyal mtshan,* 1764-1853)

*Commentary on (Maitreya's) "Ornament for the Great Vehicle Sūtras": Blossoming Flower of the Subduer's Teaching*

mdo sde'i rgyan gyi 'grel pa thub bstan rgyas pa'i me tog

*Collected Works of Dbal-maṅ Dkon-mchog-rgyal-mtshan,* vol. 8 (*nya*), 1-375. New Delhi: Gyeltan Gelek Namgyal, 1974.